KU-020-306

REASONS
WHY WE
SHOULD CONSIDER
CHRISTIANITY

For more information about the ministry of Campus Crusade for Christ, write to:

England:	Campus Crusade for Christ 4 Temple Row Birmingham B2 5HG
Australia:	LIFE PO Box A399 Sydney South 2000
Canada:	Campus Crusade for Christ Box 300 Vancouver, B.C. V6C 2X3
New Zealand:	Lay Institute for Evangelism PO Box 8786 Auckland 3
West Africa:	Great Commission Movement of Nigeria PO Box 500 Jos, Plateau State Nigeria
Republic of South Africa:	Life Ministry PO Box/Bus 91015 Auckland Park 2006
USA:	Campus Crusade for Christ International Arrowhead Springs, San Bernardino CA 92414
Ireland:	Campus Crusade for Christ 264 Merrion Road Dublin 4

JOSH MCDOWELL
and DON STEWART

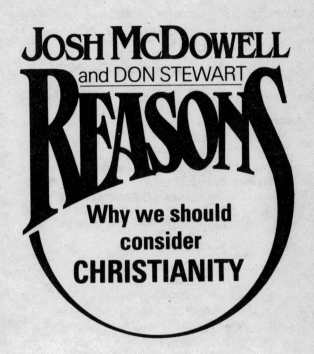

REASONS

Why we should consider CHRISTIANITY

Scripture Press **SP**

Amersham-on-the-Hill, Bucks HP6 6JQ, England

Copyright © 1981 Campus Crusade for Christ Inc, USA.

Published in the USA by
HERE'S LIFE PUBLISHERS INC,
PO Box 1576, San Bernardino, CA 92402.

First British edition 1988

All rights reserved.
No part of this publication may be reproduced or
transmitted, in any form or by any means, electronic
or mechanical, including photocopy, recording, or
any information, storage and retrieval system, without
permission in writing from the publisher.

ISBN 0 946515 52 2

Scripture quotations are taken from the
New American Standard Bible (NASB) unless
otherwise noted.

A Campus Crusade for Christ book,
designed and printed in Great Britain for
SCRIPTURE PRESS FOUNDATION (UK) LTD
Raans Road, Amersham-on-the-Hill, Bucks HP6 6JQ by
Nuprint Ltd, Harpenden, Herts AL5 4SE

CONTENTS ∎

INTRODUCTION ■

'What does it mean that the Bible is inspired?', 'Is the solar system really 4.5 million years old?' These are some of the questions that those who aren't Christians ask. This book has been written to give answers to such questions.

Over 50 questions are covered, dealing with the subjects of the Bible ('Is everything in the Bible to be taken literally?'), through evolution and creation ('Is there evidence of instantaneous creation?', 'Who is man's ancestor?'), to what it really means to become a Christian.

Written by the experienced lecturers Josh McDowell and Don Stewart, the book argues that the Christian faith is both reasonable and valid. The authors present concise answers, and at the end of each section books for further reading are given, for those who want to pursue subjects in more detail.

THE BIBLE ■

Introduction

After *Answers* was released we were inundated
with many questions that we had not had space
to answer. Many of the inquiries centered
around why we believe the Old and New
Testaments are the very word of God—a verbal
propositional revelation by God Himself.

Many readers have expressed an interest in
the various translations and paraphrases of the
Bible. Why so many translations? Which one is
best? What about the Textus Receptus? These
are some of the questions posed.

The historical reliability and accuracy of the
Bible was dealt with in two previous books,
Evidence That Demands a Verdict and *More
Evidence That Demands a Verdict*.

Reasons Skeptics Should Consider Christianity
is written to give various reasons why we
believe in the inspiration of the Bible as God's
message to man.

This work also treats another issue of great
interest today. Is the theory of evolution the
best scientific model to explain the origins of
man and the universe? This is a question that
has occupied the thinking of both the lay and
scholarly worlds. This section deals with forty
reasons why we question the theory of evolution
as being the best scientific explanation of the

facts involved in the science/creation controversy.

This book is not meant to be a scholarly treatise, rather it has been written to increase the understanding of the average person.

What does it mean, the Bible is inspired?

The inspiration of the Bible is an extremely crucial topic in today's world. Many talk about the Bible being inspired. But when asked to define what they mean by inspiration, they give a variety of definitions.

Some contend the Bible is inspired in the same way as all great literature. "It challenges the human heart to reach new heights," they say. However, this does not make the Bible unique. Many other books, including those of Shakespeare, Milton, Homer and Dickens, have produced similar results. In other words, they see the Bible as only a human literary masterpiece, not as being divine in origin.

Others believe the Bible is inspired because it *contains* the Word of God—along with myths, mistakes and legends. These people hold that it is wrong to identify the Bible as the Word of God; rather, it is a witness of God speaking to mankind. Putting it another way, the Word of God can be found in the Bible but the Word of God is not synonymous with the Bible.

Two important verses speak to the heart of the matter: 2 Timothy 3:16 and 2 Peter 1:21. The former reads, "All Scripture is inspired by God and profitable for teaching, for reproof, for correction, for training in righteousness." The word *inspired* is a translation of the Greek word *theopneustos,* meaning God-breathed. Thus the origin of Scripture is God, not man; it is God-breathed.

The second verse, 2 Peter 1:21, says, "For no prophecy was ever made by an act of human will, but men moved by the Holy Spirit spoke from God." This also confirms that the writers were moved by God to record that which God desired. Mechanical dictation was not employed as some claim. Rather, God used each individual writer and his personality to accomplish a divinely authoritative work.

The process of inspiration extended to every word ("all Scripture"), refuting the idea of myth and error. Since God is behind the writings, and since He is perfect, the result must be infallible. If it were not infallible, we could be left with God-inspired error. It is important to understand this concept, for the entire Christian faith is based upon the premise that "God is there and He is not silent," as the late theologian Francis Schaeffer so often said.

Sometimes it is easier to understand the concept of inspiration when it is compared with revelation. Revelation relates to the origin and actual giving of truth (1 Corinthians 2:10). Inspiration, on the other hand, relates to the receiving and actual recording of truth.

Inspiration means that "God the Holy Spirit worked in a unique *supernatural* way so that the written words of the Scripture writers were also the words of God."

The human authors of Scripture wrote spontaneously using their own minds and experiences, yet their words were not merely the words of men but actually the words of God. God's control was always with them in their writings with the result being the Bible—the Word of God in the words of men.

To what extent is the Bible inspired?

If a person recognizes that the Bible is the inspired Word of God, he often questions the degree of inspiration. Does it include every book, every word? Does it extend to historical matters? How about scientific statements? Does it include manuscript copies and translations?

A classic statement on the extent of inspiration is given by B. B. Warfield, a reformed theologian:

The Church has held from the beginning that the Bible is the Word of God in such a sense that its words, though written and bearing indelibly impressed upon them the marks of their human origin, were written, nevertheless, under such an influence of the Holy Ghost as to be also the words of God, the adequate expression of His mind and will. It has always recognized that this conception of co-authorship implies that the Spirit's superintendence extends to the choice of the words by the human authors (verbal inspiration, but not a mechanical dictation!) and preserves its product from everything inconsistent with a divine authorship—thus securing, among other things, that entire truthfulness which is everywhere presupposed in and asserted for Scripture by the biblical writers (inerrancy).

The doctrine of plenary inspiration holds that the original documents of the Bible were written by men, who, though permitted to exercise their own personalities and literary talents, yet wrote under the control and guidance of the Spirit of God, the result being in every word of the original documents a perfect and errorless recording of the exact message which God desired to give to man (*The Inspiration and Authority of the Bible*, p. 173).

Two words describe the extent of inspiration according to the Bible: verbal and plenary.

Plenary means full, complete, extending to all parts. The Apostle Paul says in 2 Timothy 3:16, "All Scripture is inspired of God." And Paul told the Thessalonians, "For this reason we also constantly thank God that when you received from us the word of God's message, you accepted it not as the word of men, but for what it really is, the Word of God" (1 Thessalonians 2:13).

The Bible ends with this warning, "I testify to everyone who hears the words of the prophecy of this book: if anyone adds to them, God shall add to him the plagues which are written in this book; and if anyone takes away from the words of the book of this prophecy, God shall take away his part from the tree of life and from the holy city, which are written in this book" (Revelation 22:18, 19).

The entire Bible is inspired, not just certain parts!

Inspiration extends not only to all parts of the Bible; it extends to the very words, "which things we also speak, not in words taught by human wisdom, but in those taught by the Spirit, combining spiritual thoughts with spiritual words"(1 Corinthians 2:13).

Sometimes the biblical writers base their arguments on a particular expression or a single word. For example, in Galatians 3:16 the Apostle Paul cites Genesis 13:15 and 17:8 when God said to Abraham, "Unto your seed

(*descendant*) will I give this land," not unto
your descendants, plural. Paul's whole argument
is based on the noun being singular rather than
plural. Rene Pache, in *The Inspiration and
Authority of Scripture* (p. 77), gives a pertinent
summary of this idea. We may agree with him
that "very often the meaning of a whole
passage rests entirely on one word, a singular or
a plural number, the tense of a verb, the details
of a prophecy, the precision of a promise and
the silence of the text on a certain point."

It is of monumental importance to identify
the extent of inspiration to include every book
of Scripture, each part of every book, and
every word in each book as given in the
original. This does not include any manuscript
copy or any translation which is a reproduction.

No one manuscript or translation is inspired,
only the original. However, for all intents and
purposes, they are virtually inspired since, with
today's great number of manuscripts available
for scrutiny, the science of textual criticism can
render us an adequate representation.
Therefore, we can be assured that when we
read the Bible we are reading the inspired Word
of God.

Charles Wesley, one of the founders of
Methodism, wrote,

The Bible must be the invention either of good men or
angels, bad men or devils, or of God. Therefore:

1. It could not be the invention of good men or angels, for
   they neither would or could make a book, and tell lies all
   the time they were writing it, saying, "Thus saith the
   Lord," when it was their own invention.
2. It could not be the invention of bad men or devils, for
   they would not make a book which commands all duty,

forbids all sin, and condemns their souls to hell to all
eternity.
3. Therefore, I draw this conclusion, that the Bible must be
given by divine inspiration. (Robert W. Burtner and
Robert E. Chiles, *A Compendium of Wesley's Theology*,
p. 20.)

The evidence that the *very words* of the Bible
are God-given may be briefly summarized as
follows:

- This is the claim of the classical text
  (2 Timothy 3:16).
- It is the emphatic testimony of Paul that he
  spoke in "Words . . . taught by the Spirit"
  (1 Corinthians 2:13).
- It is evident from the repeated formula, "It is
  written."
- Jesus said that which was written in the whole
  Old Testament spoke of Him (Luke 24:27, 44;
  John 5:39; Hebrews 10:7).
- The New Testament constantly equates the
  Word of God with the Scripture (writings of
  the Old Testament (cf. Matthew 21:42;
  Romans 15:4; 2 Peter 3:16).
- Jesus indicated that not even the smallest part
  of a Hebrew word or letter could be broken
  (Matthew 5:18).
- The New Testament refers to the written
  record as the "oracles of God" (Romans 3:2;
  Hebrews 5:12).
- Occasionally the writers were even told to
  "diminish not a word" (Jeremiah 26:2, AV).
  John even pronounced an anathema on all
  who would add to or subtract from the
  "words of the prophecy of this book"
  (Revelation 22:18, 19).

How could fallible men produce an infallible Bible?

One of the most frequent arguments leveled against the infallibility of the Bible is based upon the fact that the Bible was written by human authors. Human beings are fallible. Since the Bible was written by these fallible human beings, it necessarily follows that the Bible is fallible. Or so the argument goes. As Roman Catholic theologian Bruce Vawter writes, "A human literature containing no error would indeed be a contradiction in terms, since nothing is more human than to err" (*Biblical Inspiration*, Philadelphia: Westminster, 1972).

Although we often hear this accusation, it just is not correct. We grant that human beings do make mistakes, and that they make them often. But they do not necessarily make mistakes in all cases, and they do not necessarily have to make mistakes.

For example, several years ago one of the authors was teaching a class on the reliability of the Bible. For it, he had typed up a one-page outline of the course. The finished product was inerrant; it had no typographical errors, no mistakes in copying from the hand-written original. Although the author was human and was prone to make mistakes, he was in fact infallible in this instance.

The point is this: It is not impossible for a human being to perform a mistake-free act. It is not impossible for fallible man to correctly record both sayings and events. Thus to rule out the possibility of an inerrant Bible by appealing to the fallibility of men does not hold up.

John Warwick Montgomery, lawyer/ theologian, illustrates this truth:

The directions for operating my washing machine, for example, are literally infallible; if I do just what they say, the machine will respond. Euclid's *Geometry* is a book of perfect internal consistency; grant the axioms and the proofs follow inexorably. From such examples (and they could readily be multiplied) we must conclude that human beings, though they often err, need not err in all particular instances.

To be sure, the production over centuries of sixty-six inerrant and mutually consistent books by different authors is a tall order—and we cheerfully appeal to God's Spirit to achieve it—but the point remains that there is nothing metaphysically inhuman or against human nature in such a possibility. If there were, have we considered the implications for Christology? The incarnate Christ, as a real man, would also have had to err; and we have already seen that error in His teachings would totally negate the revelational value of the incarnation, leaving man as much in the dark as to the meaning of life and salvation as if no incarnation had occurred at all (*God's Inerrant Word*, p. 33).

We also believe that there is sufficient evidence that the Bible is the infallible Word of God. The Scriptures themselves testify, "All Scripture is God-breathed" (2 Timothy 3:16). If they contain error then one must call it God-inspired error. This is totally incompatible with the nature of God as revealed in the Bible. For example, Titus 1:2 says God cannot lie. John 17:17 says, "Thy word is truth."

Examples could be multiplied. The testimony of Scripture is clear. God used fallible men to receive and record His infallible Word so that it would reach us, correct and without error. Sounds difficult? With our God it's not. As He said (Jeremiah 32:27), "Behold, I am the Lord, the God of all flesh; is anything too difficult for Me?"

How do you know that the writings of the Apostle Paul were inspired?

Saul of Tarsus, who upon his conversion became the Apostle Paul, wrote at least twelve letters which have been included in the New Testament. Why should we accept this man's writing as being God's Word?

Paul claimed that he was "an apostle, not from men, neither through men, but through Jesus Christ and God the Father" (Galatians 1:1). He was an apostle, one who had seen the risen Christ. "Am I not an apostle?" he asks rhetorically. "Have I not seen Jesus our Lord?" (1 Corinthians 9:1). He was, therefore, in a position of authority in the early church.

The apostle also received a unique revelation from God. "The gospel which was preached by me . . . is not after man. For neither did I receive it from man, nor was I taught it, but it came through revelation of Jesus Christ," he says (Galatians 1:11, 12). This calling was given to the apostle at his birth: "It was the good pleasure of God, who separated me, even from my mother's womb . . . to reveal His Son in me" (Galatians 1:15, 16).

This divine message which Paul received was transmitted correctly to both the churches and the individuals to whom he wrote. He tells Titus, "God, who cannot lie, . . . in His own seasons manifested His word in the message, wherewith I was entrusted according to the commandment of God our Savior" (Titus 1:2, 3).

He went on to say, "For our exhortation does not come from error or impurity or by way of deceit; but just as we have been approved by God to be entrusted with the gospel, so we speak, not as pleasing men but God, who examines our heart" (1 Thessalonians 2:3, 4).

The revelation given to Paul was a yardstick by which to gauge other so-called revelations: "If any man is preaching to you a gospel contrary to that which you received, let him be accursed" (Galatians 1:8). His message bore the stamp of divine authority: "If anyone thinks he is a prophet or spiritual, let him recognize that the things which I write to you are the Lord's commandment" (1 Corinthians 14:37).

In Paul's first letter to the Thessalonians, he made his authority crystal clear: "And for this reason we also constantly thank God that when you received from us the word of God's message, you accepted it not as the word of men, but for what it really is, the word of God, which also performs its work in you who believe" (1 Thessalonians 2:13). "Thus, he who rejects this is not rejecting men but God" (1 Thessalonians 4:8).

The disciple Simon Peter confirmed the fact that Paul's writings were of divine authority: "And regard the patience of our Lord to be salvation; just as also our beloved brother Paul, according to the wisdom given him wrote to you, as also in all his letters, speaking in them of these things hard to understand, which the untaught and unstable distort, as they do also the rest of the Scriptures, to their own destruction" (2 Peter 3:15, 16).

Therefore, we have proof that Paul, who was called by the Lord Jesus Christ Himself on the Damascus road, writes with the authority of God. He was God's chosen instrument to reveal the mysteries of Christ Jesus, for without his writings, the explanation of the death and resurrection of Christ would be incomplete.

Since Jesus was human, was He not also fallible?

Jesus of Nazareth was a human being. Since human beings are limited in their knowledge, does this not mean that Jesus also was limited? Should we not dismiss His statements as being conditioned by His own time? Granted, He said some magnificent things. But why should we accept His word seeing that He was human?

Questions such as these often come up when we talk about the person of Jesus Christ. People will point to Jesus' own statements to show that he was ignorant of some things.

When Jesus was asked about the time of His second coming, He responded, "But of that day and that hour knoweth no man, no, not the angels which are in heaven, neither the Son, but the Father" (Mark 13:32, KJV).

Once when surrounded by a crowd, Jesus was touched by someone. As a result, He turned to the crowd and asked, "Who touched my clothes?" (Mark 5:30), thus supposedly revealing His ignorance. Furthermore, He asked questions of people, "What is your name?"

(Mark 5:9), "How many loaves do you have?" (Mark 6:38).

These passages reveal that Christ did not know certain things, skeptics say. Why, then, trust any of His statements?

The New Testament answers the question, "Was Christ fallible?" with a resounding, no! It must be remembered that Jesus had two natures, one human, one divine. As a man, there were things of which He was ignorant. But as God, He possessed all knowledge.

Jesus was not a man who worked Himself up to the position of being God. Rather, He was God condescending to humanity. Philippians 2:5-11 states that, as God, Jesus chose to lay aside his independent exercise of certain attributes that were rightly His. As a man, He totally trusted God the Father and lived a perfect, sinless life.

Even though He was still God while here on earth. He voluntarily laid aside certain rights He possessed. There is no hint that His statements—whether theological, historical or of some other nature—were in any way fallible.

Jesus always told the truth. When He said He did not know something He made us aware of that. Since He told us when He did not know something, we naturally can assume that when He did tell us something it was because He did know it. The fact that Christ admitted He was unaware of certain things makes us all the more secure in the statements which He made without any qualification.

Also remember that some of Jesus' questions, such as in John 6:5 and Mark 6:38, were not for His own information as though He did not know the answer, but to provoke those hearing

Him to come up with *their own response,* since the proper response was for their good (cf. John 6:5-6).

This is generally similar to God's questions in the Old Testament (as in Genesis 3, "Where are you?", etc.). These were asked not for His information but for the sake of those involved, who could in some way be helped by making a proper response. Or, they were simply rhetorical.

Moreover, as a human being Jesus possessed knowledge that was beyond the normal, as Norman Geisler points out in *Christian Apologetics* (pp. 358, 359): "Even in his human state Christ possessed supernormal if not supernatural knowledge of many things. He saw Nathanael under the fig tree, although he was not within normal visual distance (John 1:48). Jesus amazed the woman of Samaria with the information he knew about her private life (John 4:18-19).

"Jesus knew who would betray him in advance (John 6:64). He knew about Lazarus' death before he was told (John 11:14) and of his crucifixion and resurrection before it occurred (Mark 8:31; 9:31). Jesus had superhuman knowledge of the location of the fish (Luke 5:4).

"There is no indication from the Gospel record that Jesus' finitude deterred his ministry or teaching. Whatever the limitations to his knowledge, it was vastly beyond normal men and completely adequate for his mission and doctrinal teaching."

The Bible also makes it clear that Christ is the final authority on all matters with which He dealt. Individuals will be judged on what they do with His words. As He said, "He who rejects Me, and does not receive My sayings, has one who judges him; the word I spoke is what will judge him at the last day" (John 12:48).

His word is a sure foundation. Our lives need to be based upon it. "Therefore everyone who hears these words of Mine, and acts upon them, may be compared to a wise man, who built his house upon the rock," Jesus said (Matthew 7:24, NASB). His words are eternal: "Heaven and earth will pass away, but My words shall not pass away" (Matthew 24:34).

Even from these few statements it is clear that any human limitation that Jesus submitted to was not reflected in His theological statements and teachings. One cannot use this as a viable excuse for rejecting the finality of Jesus' statements. He has demonstrated the fact that He has authority to claim infallibility by returning from the dead the third day (Romans 1:4).

Although Jesus was truly God, He was also truly man. Or you could say He was just as much man as if He had never been God, and He was just as much God as if He had never been man. He was the God-man.

It is now up to each individual to choose whether to build his house on the rock or on the sand.

How did Jesus view the Old Testament?

We could cite many reasons for the Old Testament being God's Word, but the strongest argument comes from the Lord Jesus Himself. As God in human flesh, Jesus speaks with final authority. And His testimony regarding the Old Testament is loud and clear.

Jesus believed that the Old Testament was divinely inspired, the veritable Word of God. He said, "The Scripture cannot be broken" (John 10:35). He referred to Scripture as "the commandment of God" (Matthew 15:3) and as the "Word of God" (Matthew 15:6). He also indicated that it was indestructible: "Until Heaven and earth pass away, not the smallest letter or stroke shall pass away from the law, until all is accomplished" (Matthew 5:18). Notice that He mentions even the words and letters!

When dealing with the people of His day, whether it was with the disciples or religious rulers, Jesus constantly referred to the Old Testament: "Have you not read that which was spoken to you by God?" (Matthew 22:31); "Yea; and have you never read, 'Out of the mouth of infants and nursing babes thou hast prepared praise for thyself'?" (Matthew 21:16, citing Psalm 8:2); and "Have you not read what David did?" (Matthew 12:3). Examples could be multipled to demonstrate that Jesus was conversant with the Old Testament and its content. He quoted from it often and He trusted it totally.

He confirmed many of the accounts in the Old Testament, such as the destruction of

Sodom and the death of Lot's wife (Luke 17:29, 32), the murder of Abel by his brother Cain (Luke 11:51), the calling of Moses (Mark 12:26), the manna given in the wilderness (John 6:31-51), the judgment upon Tyre and Sidon (Matthew 11:32), and many others.

Not only did Jesus confirm the historicity of these accounts, He also authenticated some of the passages that are most disputed today. Many modern scholars do not believe that Moses wrote the first five books of the Old Testament, but Jesus did (see Matthew 19:8, 9; John 7:19; Mark 12:29-31).

Some modern scholars also assume the existence of more than one Isaiah, but Jesus believed in only one. In Luke 4:17-21, He cites Isaiah 61:1, 2 (the so-called second Isaiah or Deutero-Isaiah) while in Matthew 15:7-9 He refers to the first part of Isaiah's work (Isaiah 6:9) without the slightest hint of more than one author.

The account of Daniel is rejected today by many as actually coming from the pen of Daniel, but the Lord Jesus believed him to be a prophet (Matthew 24:15). The account of Adam and Eve often is ridiculed today as legend, but Jesus believed the story to be true (Matthew 19:1-6).

Likewise, the narrative of Noah and the great flood not only is authenticated by Jesus (Matthew 24:37), it also is used as an example of His second coming. Finally, the most unbelievable of all—the account of Jonah and the great fish— is used by Jesus as a sign of His resurrection (Matthew 12:39ff).

It almost seems as though Jesus was

anticipating twentieth century biblical criticism when He authenticated these accounts. The conclusion is simple. If a person believes in Jesus Christ he should be consistent and believe that the Old Testament and its accounts are correct. Many want to accept Jesus, but also want to reject a large portion of the Old Testament. This option is not available. Either Jesus knew what He was talking about or He did not. The evidence is clear that Jesus saw the Old Testament as being God's Word; His attitude toward it was nothing less than total trust.

Didn't Jesus accommodate His teachings to the beliefs of His day?

One of the most popular theories about the life of Christ is alleged accommodation to error. This idea allows one to "have his cake and eat it, too" for it says that Jesus accommodated His teaching to the Jewish traditions that were current during His time. These traditions concern beliefs about authorship, inspiration, historical accuracy and the basic truthfulness of the Old Testament.

For example, this theory holds that Jesus did not actually believe that God destroyed Sodom and Gomorrah (Matthew 11:23, 24), or that the people on the earth at the time of Noah perished in a great flood (Matthew 24:37-39), or that Jonah was really in the belly of the great fish (Matthew 12:39-41). It was not the purpose of Christ, they claim, to teach historical truth or to question it. His purpose was to teach spiritual truth. Therefore, any mention of historical personages or events does not mean that Jesus believed them to be true.

This theory, though widespread, has several problems that make it impossible. For one thing, it destroys the entire thrust of the Bible, namely that God acted in historical situations to bring His saving message to mankind. The Bible asserts that man is responsible for believing the biblical message because the events and miracles actually did occur.

Jesus said, "Woe to you, Chorazin! Woe to you, Bethsaida! For if the miracles had occurred in Tyre and Sidon which occurred in you they would have repented long ago in sackcloth and ashes. Nevertheless I say to you, it shall be more tolerable for Tyre and Sidon in the day of judgment, than for you" (Matthew 11:21, 22).

Now if there was not any judgment on Tyre and Sidon, the warnings of Jesus to Chorazin and Bethsaida were meaningless. This holds true for the other accounts in the Old Testament that Jesus alluded to when making a comparison (Jonah and the resurrection, Noah and the second coming, etc.). If these accounts have no factual basis, then any objective meaning to the biblical comparisons is gone and the door to agnosticism and atheism swings wide open.

How could we know that there exists any basis of belief for the spiritual and theological statements Jesus made if we cannot trust His statements of a historical nature? How could an individual know what statements to believe and

what statements Jesus only accommodated to
His audience? Moreover, if we allow for some
of the historical statements to be an
accommodation, why not allow some of the
ethical statements to be merely an
accommodation to a primitive Jewish belief?

It is easy to see how one could be led to
agnosticism by following this theory to its
logical end, for eventually one would be
hard-pressed to come up with some standard to
determine what is the real belief of Jesus and
what is only an accommodation to the people of
His day. We could never be sure exactly what
Jesus believed.

Furthermore, this idea of accommodation
contradicts everything we know about the
character of Jesus. When confronted with error,
Jesus always was quick to rebuke it, whether it
was false ideas about God or misconceptions
about what the Bible teaches (Matthew 15;
Mark 7).

The strongest rebuke in all of Scripture is
found in Matthew 23 when Jesus denounces the
false religious leaders of His day and their
unbiblical practices. This denunciation was
totally opposed to the current thought of the
day in which Christ lived.

The religious leaders believed that God would
be pleased with their legalistic emphasis on
keeping the letter of the Law, but Jesus pointed
out that God desired them to keep the spirit of
the Law. Therefore, He labeled them
hypocrites, snakes, and children of hell. This is
hardly compatible with any theory of
accommodation.

Finally, the accommodation theory gives a

very low view of Christ. Jesus said, "I am the truth" (John 14:6). The theory holds that His life and ministry consisted of telling only half-truths, holding back that which He knew was incorrect. This would mean that Jesus allowed the end to justify the means, something that His life and ministry simply did not do. If Jesus did not tell the whole truth, He did not tell the truth at all.

In conclusion, we believe the words of Jesus aptly sum up the matter: "If I told you earthly things and you do not believe, how shall you believe if I tell you heavenly things?" (John 3:12).

Many interpret the Bible allegorically. Why do you interpret it literally?

Although some view the Bible as an allegory, we believe a literal interpretation is the only interpretation that does justice to the facts. There are several reasons for accepting the Bible literally.

The Bible purports to be the Word of God. Over and over we find such phrases as "the Word of the Lord came unto Moses," "God spoke," "thus saith the Lord."

When God spoke, it was in real-life situations, not in some never-never land. The Bible views itself as a non-fiction book. When the writers cite other persons or events in Scripture, they cite them as real, not imaginary or allegorical.

For example, Jesus referred to Jonah

(Matthew 12:39ff) as a sign of His resurrection. The writer to the Hebrews cites many great Old Testament men and women of faith (Hebrews 11) as examples to the believer. Nowhere is the story of Abraham or Samson looked at in any way but factual. Thus the Bible itself gives a witness that it should be taken at face value. Scripture interprets Scripture literally.

The nature of God, as revealed in the Bible, makes it clear that He has the ability to communicate with people. Since God created mankind for the purpose of establishing a relationship, it naturally follows that He would use an understandable method. Consequently, we do not need to look for some strange hidden meaning to what the Scripture says for it is very plain.

An example of this would be God's judgment on the wicked whose end God has made clear: ". . . when the Lord Jesus shall be revealed from Heaven with His mighty angels in flaming fire, dealing out retribution to those who do not know God and to those who do not obey the gospel of our Lord Jesus Christ. And these will pay the penalty of eternal destruction, away from the presence of the Lord and from the glory of His power" (2 Thessalonians 1:7-9).

It also is important to realize that the Bible is aimed at mankind. The people were given the responsibility to heed what God had revealed, and they were expected to take God at His word: "You shall follow the Lord your God and fear Him; and you shall keep His command- ments, listen to His voice, serve Him and cling to Him" (Deuteronomy 13:4).

Any message from a so-called prophet had to

be tested against what God had objectively and literally said: "Beloved, do not believe every spirit, but test the spirits to see whether they are from God: because many false prophets are gone out into the world. By this you know the Spirit of God: every Spirit that confesses that Jesus Christ has come in the flesh is from God" (1 John 4:1, 2).

There is no double-talk or weasel-wording in Scripture. The message is clear, and God expects mankind to act responsibly on what He has revealed. The excuse so many people use, that the Bible can be understood so many ways and that everyone has his own interpretation, just is not true. The issue has been made very clear: "He who believes in the Son has eternal life; but He who does not obey the Son shall not see life, but the wrath of God abides on him" (John 3:36).

Is everything in the Bible to be taken literally?

When we say that we take the Bible literally, we do not mean that figurative language is absent from the Bible. However, to interpret figuratively we must find a good reason in the passage to justify doing this.

Some types of writing by their very nature tend to exclude the possibility of figurative language. These include laws, historical writings, and philosophic writings although even these have figurative language where it is sensible. For example, "Martin Luther was like a bull in a china shop." Some literature (poetry, for example) also is figurative in nature.

A good rule for interpretation is, "If the literal sense makes good sense, seek no other sense lest you come up with nonsense." The words of a given text should be interpreted literally if possible. If not possible, one should move to figurative language.

Usually there are clues in the context. Sometimes there will be a definition. For example, when the Book of Revelation speaks of the dragon (Revelation 12:9), the dragon is defined for the reader. Knowing the culture also will help, for the more one knows about the language and thought forms of a particular period, the better chance one will have to determine how to interpret a given passage.

Many have built a straw man out of the teaching of literal interpretation, alleging that we have to take everything in the Bible literally, e.g., "the trees of the field shall clap their hands" (Isaiah 55:12).

The Bible contains definite types of figurative language, including metaphor, simile, hyperbole, and anthropomorphism. A metaphor is a comparison by direct statement. In John 15:1 Jesus states, "I am the true vine." This does not mean He is a literal vine, but that He can be compared to one.

A simile is a comparison by use of the words "like" or "as." Exodus 24:17 states, "The glory of the Lord was like a consuming fire on the moutain top."

A hyperbole is an exaggeration for emphasis. In John 21:25 we find an example of this: "And there are also many other things which Jesus did, which if they were written in detail, I suppose that even the world itself would not contain the books which were written."

Anthropomorphism, which is found particularly in the Old Testament, is attributing to God human characteristics or experiences. This can be seen in statements such as "It repented the Lord that He had made man" (Genesis 6:6, KJV), and "The eyes of the Lord move to and fro throughout the earth that He may strongly support those whose heart is completely His" (2 Chronicles 16:9).

However, many statements previously thought to be figurative have, with greater knowledge, proven to be quite literal. Take, for example, the snake eating dust. Research has shown that snakes do eat dust. It helps them to navigate—they "see" through the dust they ingest.

Therefore, figurative language does have a place in Scripture, but only when certain factors indicate that the passage in question is not to be interpreted literally.

Which version of the Bible should I use?

We are constantly asked about the virtues and limitations of different Bible translations. The following section contains an evaluation of the major English translations and paraphrases that are used today.

At this point we should explain what is meant by the terms *translation* and *paraphrase*. Simply stated, a translation is an attempt to convey into one language what another language literally says. In the case of the New Testament, a translation attempts to bring out as accurately as possible what the original Greek text *says*.

A paraphrase, on the other hand, says something in different words from those the author originally used. Ideally, a paraphrase attempts to bring out exactly what the original author *meant*.

An example of each will clarify the difference:

TRANSLATION
In the beginning was the Word, and the Word was with God, and the Word was God. The same was in the beginning with God (John 1:1, 2, KJV).

PARAPHRASE
Before anything else existed there was Christ, with God. He has always been alive and is himself God (John 1:1, 2, TLB).

Therefore, in a translation the emphasis is upon what was literally said, while a paraphrase emphasizes what the paraphraser believes to be the original meaning.

KING JAMES VERSION

History. When Elizabeth, Queen of England, died in 1603, her crown went to James I. Soon after his ascendancy to the throne, James brought church leaders to Hampton Court to discuss the state of the church.

From their meeting a notable resolution was adopted:

"That a translation be made of the whole

Bible, as consonant as can be to the original Hebrew and Greek; and this to be set out and printed, without marginal notes, and only to be used in all churches of England in time of Divine Service."

This resolution set in motion the most successful of all English translations of the Bible, the King James Version of 1611, also known as the Authorized Version.

Purpose. The purpose of the King James Version can be found in the preface, "The translators to the reader: Truly, good Christian Reader, we never thought from the beginning that we should need to make a new translation, nor yet to make a bad one a good one: . . . But to make a good one better, or out of many good ones one principal good one."

The basis for the new translation was the Bishops Bible (completed in 1568).

Unique Features. The flowery dedication to James I, still printed in many editions, is a unique part of this translation. Many mistakenly think that James I was one of the translators when, in fact, he merely organized and approved the translation.

One unexplained feature is the cessation of the paragraph marks after Acts 20:36. For some unknown reason they stop at this point.

In the history of the printing of the KJV some unique mistakes arose. In the 1631 edition, the word "not" was omitted from the commandment, "Thou shalt not commit adultery." This led to a fine of 300 pounds against the King's printers. The 1795 translation of Mark 7:27 read, "Let the children first be killed" (rather than "filled").

Value and Limitations. The King James Version is unsurpassed in its sheer beauty and literary value, a masterpiece of the seventeenth century English language in which it was written. Unfortunately, this seventeenth century language is the language of a bygone era.

Many words found in the KJV are obsolete today, while others have a totally different meaning than they did then. Moreover, discoveries have been made in the last 350 years in the field of linguistics, history and archaeology that justify further translations of the Bible.

Indeed the King James Version was itself a mere revision of the Bishops Bible, not a new translation. As new knowledge came to light, and the English language changed, the church felt obligated to produce a more accurate translation of the Word of God. Revision and correction of past translations was thought not only desirable, but absolutely necessary to communicate the Word of God.

REVISED VERSION

History. The publication of the King James Version of 1611 did not mark the end of new translations of the Bible. Sixteen years after the release of the Authorized Version, a fifth century Greek manuscript (*Codex Alexandrinus*) was brought to England.

This manuscript was centuries closer in time to the writing of the New Testament than the

handful of manuscripts used to translate the
Authorized Version. Moreover, the Greek
Codex Alexandrinus was different in certain
respects than the text which was used to
translate the King James.

During the next two and one half centuries, a
great number of other new manuscripts were
discovered, some dating as early as the middle
of the 4th century (*Codex Vaticanus*, A.D. 325;
Codex Siniaticus, A.D. 350).

With these discoveries and a refining of the
science of textual criticism, it was inevitable,
and even desirable, that voices would cry out
for a revision of the King James Version. The
work of revision began February 10, 1870, with
the stated intention of updating and correcting
both the text behind the KJV and the
translation from that text.

Purpose. The purpose for this revision was
revealed in a report submitted on May 3, 1870,
by the Canterbury Committee:

1. That it is desirable that a revision of the Authorized
   Version of the Holy Scriptures be undertaken.
2. That the revision be so conducted as to comprise both
   marginal renderings and such emendations as it may be
   found necessary to insert in the text of the Authorized
   Version.
3. That in the above resolutions we do not contemplate any
   new translation of the Bible, or any alteration of the
   language, except when in the judgment of the most
   competent scholars such change is necessary.
4. That in such necessary changes, the style of the language
   employed in the existing version be closely followed.
5. That it is desirable that Convocation should nominate a
   body of its own members to undertake the work of
   revision, who shall be at liberty to invite the co-operation

of any eminent for scholarship, to whatever nation or
religious body they may belong.

It is important to note that this work was to
be a revison of the King James Version, not a
new translation. Any changes from the King
James were to be done only when absolutely
necessary. Moreover, any alteration of the text
was to be indicated in the margin.

If such evidence warranted a change, the
approval of at least two-thirds of the revisers
was required before it would be incorporated
into the text. The actual number of changes far
exceeded the original expectations of the
committee, but most of the numerous changes
were merely grammatical (i.e., word order,
sentence structure).

The task of revision was completed with the
publication of the New Testament in 1881 and
the complete Bible in 1885.

Unique Features. The most striking fact about
the Revised Version is not the translation but
that the revisers departed from the Greek text
used by the King James translators. They
substituted a modified text based upon the
principles developed by Brooke Foss Westcott
and Fenton John Anthony Hort.

The use of the Westcott-Hort text led to the
omission or relegation to the margin of not a
few familiar passages, including Mark 16:9-20;
John 5:3, 4; Acts 8:37 and 1 John 5:7.
Naturally, as one would expect, there was a
certain amount of public outcry concerning
these alterations of the King James Version.
The opposition to the revision was led by John
Burgon, Dean of Chichester, who wrote

vociferously against such changes and omissions
(*The Revision Revised,* London 1883).

Value and Limitations. The great value of the
Revised Version is that it set a precedent for
further translations which could incorporate the
latest manuscript and linguistic and historical
evidence into their versions.

No single translation is perfect, and as new
discoveries come to light improvements can and
should be made. The Revised Version has
limited value in the fact that it does not have
the advantage of the great linguistic advances
and manuscript discoveries of the twentieth
century. Moreover, the revisers leaned too
heavily on the Westcott-Hort theory of textual
criticism which has been seriously challenged in
the twentieth century. Although upon its release
the Revised Version enjoyed immediate
popularity, it is not commonly used today.

AMERICAN STANDARD VERSION

History. While the revision committee in
England was busily going about its work on the
King James Version, in America a group of
thirty men was selected in 1871 to review the
work of the English revisers and offer
constructive suggestions. Any suggested change
made by the American committee was to be
considered by their British counterparts.
However, only those which received a
two-thirds vote of approval were incorporated
into the text. The remaining suggestions were
put into an appendix.

While some unauthorized translations
appeared soon after the publication of the

Revised Version which incorporated some of the suggestions made by the American contingent, there was no such immediate translation from the American committee.

This was based upon an agreement with the British revisers that no authorized translation would appear for at least fourteen years. Thus in August 1901, after the agreed time had elapsed, the American committee produced its own translation which became popularly known as the American Standard Version.

Purpose. Several factors led to an independent American translation: "The need for the American committee to publish a version containing their suggestions became apparent, especially since in 1881-1883 two unauthorized editions of the New Testament were published in (America) by incorporating the readings suggested by the American committee which were put in the appendix of the English Revised Version" (*Our English Bible in the Making,* Herbert Gordon May, p. 72). Moreover, the American Standard Version was more than a mere transference of their suggested changes contained in the appendix of the Revised Version.

In the preface to the American Standard Version, the translators make it clear that the appendix was in need of revision due to its hasty preparation. Furthermore, the British Revised Version contained only some of the American committee's suggestions in their appendix justifying an independent translation.

Unique Features. Several unique features set

apart the American Standard Version from its English counterpart. The American Standard Version translated the divine name, rendered "Lord" in both the King James Version and Revised Version, as "Jehovah" throughout the translation. It also uniformly changed "Holy Ghost" to "Holy Spirit," clearing up this inconsistency of the King James Version, page headings were added, and marginal notes improved.

Value and Limitations. The American Standard Version was the product of the best American scholarship of its day. It had the advantage of being published twenty years after the New Testament of the Revised Version.

Limitations exist, however, because the American Standard Version is still a product of its own time, not having the advantage of the wealth of discoveries and advances made in the twentieth century. As was the case with the Revised Version, the language was not modernized, leading to such archaic ways of stating things as, "The abjects gathered themselves together against me" (Psalm 35:15), and "He assayed to join Himself to the disciples" (Acts 9:26).

Nevertheless it was the best translation of the day and served as the basis for two other revisions, the Revised Standard Version and the New American Standard Bible. Although the American Standard Version is somewhat uncommon today, its positive contributions were widely enjoyed through these two revisions.

REVISED STANDARD VERSION

History. The history of the Revised Standard Version is neatly summed up in its preface:

Because of unhappy experiences with unauthorized publications in the two decades between 1881 and 1901, which tampered with the text of the English Revised Version in the supposed interest of the American public, the American Standard Version was copyrighted, to protect the text from unauthorized changes.

In 1928 this copyright was acquired by the International Council of Religious Education, and thus passed into the ownership of the churches of the United States and Canada which were associated in this Council through their boards of education and publication.

The Council appointed a committee of scholars to have charge of the text of the American Standard Version and to undertake inquiry as to whether further revision was necessary. For more than two years the Committee worked upon the problem of whether or not revision should be undertaken; and if so, what should be its nature and extent.

In the end the decision was reached that there is need for a thorough revision of the version of 1901, which will stay as close to the Tyndale-King James tradition as it can in the light of our present knowledge of the Hebrew and Greek texts and their meaning on the one hand, and our present understanding of English on the other.

Purpose. The Revised Standard Version, the accomplishment of American scholars, is an authorized revision of the American Standard Version of 1901. In the history of the English Bible there have been several authorized translations preceding the Revised Standard Version including the Great Bible (1539), the Bishops Bible (1568), King James Version (1611), Revised Version (1881-1885), and American Standard Version (1901). The

Revised Standard Version is a revision, not a new translation, as stated in the preface:

The Revised Standard Version is not a new translation in the language of today. It is not a paraphrase which aims at striking idioms. It is a revision which seeks to preserve all that is best in the English Bible as it has been known and used through the years. It is intended for use in public and private worship, not merely for reading and instruction.

We have resisted the temptation to use phrases that are merely current-usage, and have sought to put the message of the Bible in simple, enduring words that are worthy to stand in the great Tyndale-King James tradition. We are glad to say, with the King James translators: Truly (good Christian Reader) we never thought from the beginning, that we should need to make a new Translation, nor yet to make of a bad one a good one . . . but to make a good one better.

The New Testament was finished in 1946; the entire Bible in 1952.

Unique Features. One of the problems with the Revised Version and the American Standard Version resulted from the limitations restricting the language to that of the Elizabethan age. The Revised Standard Version had no such restrictions. The translators were given—and took—the freedom to modernize the language.

This included replacing the final "th" with "s" in the ending of verbs in the third person singular of the present tense. Thus "goeth" became "goes"; "cometh" became "comes," and "saith" was rendered "says." Other archaic expressions were updated including "it came to pass," "would fain," "peradventure," and "holden." English words that had changed meaning through the centuries also were modernized, bringing the language up-to-date.

Value and Limitations. The value of the Revised Standard Version lies in the fact that the language was brought up to current usage. The biblical story was made much more understandable to the masses. Also the translators had the advantage of the great discoveries in the study of comparative languages.

Near Eastern religious texts unearthed in the twentieth century shed much light on the meaning of certain Hebrew words, and the unearthing of Greek papyri demonstrated beyond all doubt that biblical Greek was not some unique Holy Ghost language but rather the common vernacular of the first century.

But the Revised Standard Version is not without problems. Many of the Old Testament passages which prophesy the coming of the Messiah are obscured in this version. For example, Psalm 45:6 is rendered, "Your Divine throne endures for ever and ever," rather than the better translation, "Thy throne, O God."

In Isaiah 7:14 the Revised Standard Version has, "Behold, a young woman shall conceive," rather than the better translation, "Behold, a virgin shall conceive." Since the New Testament cites both those passages as referring to the Messiah it would have been better for the Revised Standard Version to acknowledge the unity between the Testaments. These inconsistencies take away from an otherwise good translation.

PHILLIPS TRANSLATION

History. The Phillips Translation had its
beginning in London around the time of World
War II. Pastor J. B. Phillips was frustrated
because his youth groups could not understand
the King James Version. Consequently, he
made his own translation of Paul's letters,
published with the title, *Letters to Young
Churches* (1947).

Eventually, he translated the Gospels (1952),
Acts (1955), and the Book of Revelation (1957).
The complete New Testament was published in
1963, and revised in 1973. Phillips also
translated the four prophets (Amos, Hosea,
Isaiah 1-35, and Micah) in 1963.

Purpose. The Phillips Translation attempts to
modernize and update the language of the New
Testament in order to communicate with
contemporary man. This rendition attempts to
make the New Testament read as a freshly
written work, composed in the twentieth
century and dealing with current needs. Phillips
himself believed that a sign of a good
translation was that it did not sound at all like a
translation.

As Phillips indicated in his foreword, he also
desired to imagine himself in the place of the
biblical writers:

Perhaps a few words about the kind of technique which I
have adopted may be introduced here. I have found
imaginative sympathy, not so much with words as with
people, to be essential. If it is not presumptuous to say so, I
attempted, as far as I could, to think myself into the heart
and mind of Paul, for example, or of Mark or of John the
Divine. Then I tried further to imagine myself as each of

the New Testament authors writing his particular message
for the people of today.

Unique Features. The format of the Phillips
Translation is unique for modern editions of the
Scripture. There are not any verse numbers,
and each paragraph has a heading explaining its
contents.

It is also a meaning-for-meaning translation
rather than the traditional word-for-word
translation. Phillips believed that this method
was justified as he stated in his foreword
regarding words and their context. In doing this,
he also exposes his view of Scripture:

For the most part I am convinced that they had no idea that
they were writing Holy Scripture. They would be, or indeed
perhaps are, amazed to learn what meanings are sometimes
read back into their simple utterances!

Paul, for instance, writing in haste and urgency to some of
his wayward and difficult Christians, was not tremendously
concerned about dotting the i's and crossing the t's of his
message. I doubt very much whether he was even concerned
about being completely consistent with what he had already
written.

Consequently, it seems to me quite beside the point to study
his writings microscopically, as it were, and deduce hidden
meanings of which he was almost certainly unaware. His
letters are alive, and they are moving—in both senses of
that word—and their meaning can no more be appreciated
by cold minute examination than can the beauty of a bird's
flight be appreciated by dissection after its death. We have
to take these living New Testament documents in their
context.

Value and Limitations. The Phillips Translation
is valuable because it restates the New
Testament in a fresh, readable way that provides

new insights into the New Testament for even the most knowledgeable reader. The readability is enhanced by the format which contains headings for each section and omits verse numbers. The layout of this work lends itself to easy reading.

But easy reading does not necessarily signify something desirable. Phillips, contrary to the claim, presents a paraphrase, not a translation. His revised edition has improved somewhat on this weakness, but his work is still interpretive and highly questionable at points, reflecting his inadequate view of Scripture.

British expressions which sound peculiar to American ears also limit his edition in some places.

The Phillips New Testament, like The Good News Bible, is a fine way to introduce someone to the biblical story. But it should not be relied upon for critical study.

THE MODERN LANGUAGE BIBLE

History. The history of The Modern Language Bible dates back to 1945 with the publication of The Berkeley Version of the New Testament. Unlike many other major translations, The Berkeley Version New Testament was the work of one man, Gerrit Verkuyl. Under Verkuyl's direction, the Old Testament was completed in 1959.

In 1969, after Verkuyl's death, The Berkeley Version was extensively revised and published under the title, "The Modern Language Bible—The New Berkeley Version in Modern English." Although the title has been changed, the publishers insist (in the preface) that The Modern Language Bible is still The Berkeley Version:

This is still The Berkeley Version. It rests upon the foundation Dr. Verkuyl laid. Nevertheless, the numerous changes in the New Testament text, explanatory notes, and headings warrant calling this 1969 edition The Modern Language Bible—The New Berkeley Version in Modern English.

Purpose. The original purpose for The Berkeley Version was to provide the English-speaking world with an up-to-date translation in modern language:

This is not just another revision; it is a completely new translation. We have turned to the original languages of both Testaments, assured that "holy men from God spoke as they were carried along by the Holy Spirit." Neither is this a paraphrase, for that leads so readily to the infusion of human thought with divine revelation, to the confusion of the reader. Instead of paraphrasing, we offer brief notes, related to, but apart from the inspired writings, to clarify and to give a sharper view of the message.

The Modern Language Bible, appearing in 1969, sought to revise and update The Berkeley Version:

Approximately twenty-five years have passed since The Berkeley New Testament first appeared in 1945. During this quarter century, the need for its revision has become evident. As is inevitable with any Bible translation—and perhaps most of all with a one-man version—idiosyncrasies and other matters requiring correction have come to light.

Unique Features. One of the unique aspects of The Modern Language Bible is the extensive notes that accompany the text. These notes are not only highly instructive, they also are devotional. Verkuyl, along with the subsequent translators, were evangelicals who had a high regard for the Scriptures, and this is reflected in the quality of the notes.

Value and Limitations. The Modern Language Bible has many commendable features, not the least of which is its faithful rendering of the Messianic prophecies of the Old Testament (as stated in the preface to the 1959 edition):

We are in tune with the "Authorized Version" of 1611 in fidelity to the Messianic Promise, first made as soon as man had sinned, renewed to Abraham, Isaac and Jacob, narrowed to Judah's offspring and later to David's descendants. This promise remained the hope of the worshiping Hebrews, whose prophets stimulated their faith, and Jesus reminded the Emmaus pilgrims of it, "starting from Moses and through all the prophets . . . in all the Scriptures that referred to Himself." To be faithful to this everlasting Evangel we needed to be faithful to the original Scriptures.

(This is in contrast to the Revised Standard Version which, unhappily, is inconsistent in translating prophecies referring to Jesus.)

Another good feature of the Modern Language Bible is the accomplishment of its desire to be a literal translation of the Greek and Hebrew, rather than an interpretive paraphrase. The result is a faithful rendering of the original. However, in places it is too literal to be completely readable.

The notes, a product of the highest evangelical scholarship, provide great benefits to the reader. The Modern Language Bible is an excellent translation done with the highest reverence for the Scripture and can be of great value to anyone who desires to read and study the Word of God.

THE AMPLIFIED BIBLE

History. In 1965 the Amplified Bible (in one volume) appeared in print. It was the culmination of several separate volumes including The Amplified Gospel of John (1954), The Amplified New Testament (1958), and The Amplified Old Testament (in two parts: 1962, 1964).

Purpose. The Amplified Bible, far from being another translation, purports to do something no other edition has ever done.

From the days of John Wycliffe and the first English Bible down to the present time, scholarly translators have worked diligently on English versions designed to faithfully present the Scriptures in contemporary language! The Amplified Bible is not an attempt to duplicate what has already been achieved. Rather, its intent is to progress beyond the point where the others have stopped.

Its purpose is to reveal, together with the single word English equivalent to each key Hebrew and Greek word, any other clarifying shades of meaning that may be concealed by the traditional word-for-word method of translation. Now, possibly for the first time, the full meaning of the key words in the original text is available in an English version of the Bible.

Unique Features. The unique nature of The Amplified Bible is that it adds to, explains, and attempts to clarify the words of Scripture. No other edition of the Scripture attempts to bring out these expansions of the texts and shades of meaning. Other editions use the margin or footnotes to accomplish this feat, while The Amplified Bible puts it directly into the text.

Another unique feature of The Amplified Bible is the fact that the leading figure in compiling this work was a woman, Frances E. Siewert.

Value and Limitations. The value of The Amplified Bible lies in its ability to expand the meaning of the original texts. Its service is more that of a commentary than a translation.

Although The Amplified Bible can be helpful in bringing out some of the meaning of words and expressions, several weaknesses limit its effectiveness. For example, in some of the passages it is difficult to follow the thought of the writer. This is due to the added, expansive words put into the text. In this sense, the amplifications are a hindrance rather than a help.

For example, in the Sermon on the Mount, the repetition of amplifying the word "blessed" (Matthew 5:3-11) is not only unnecessary; it is monotonous.

Furthermore, The Amplified Bible suffers from the same problems as paraphrases: It is highly interpretive. The theological bias of the amplifier cannot help but show through when the meaning of words and expressions are given. Although the preparers of The Amplified Bible have a high view of the Bible, many of their "amplifications" are totally subjective and open to argumentation.

The Amplified Bible should be used only alongside a good translation, never studied by itself.

THE JERUSALEM BIBLE

History. The Jerusalem Bible has an interesting history. Its genesis is found in *La Bible de Jerusalem,* a French translation made in Jerusalem by the *Dominican Ecole Biblique et Archeologique.* This authoritative translation was completed in several volumes with extensive notes. In 1956, this French edition appeared in one volume with an abridgement of the notes. The Jerusalem Bible in English contains these notes translated from the French, with the translation itself based upon the original biblical languages.

Purpose. The editor of The Jerusalem Bible lists in his foreword two reasons for this new edition of the Holy Scriptures:

Now for Christian thinking in the twentieth century two slogans have been wisely adopted: *aggiornamento*, or keeping abreast of the times, and *approfondimento*, or deepening of theological thought. This double programme must be for the Bible too. Its first part can be carried out by translating into the language we use today, its second part by providing notes which are neither sectarian nor superficial.

Thus, the desire of the translators is to put The Jerusalem Bible in understandable language for modern man. As a further aid to Bible understanding many explanatory notes accompany the text.

Unique Features. Two things make the Jerusalem Bible unique. First, The Jerusalem Bible is the first complete Catholic Bible translated into English from the original biblical languages. (The New American Bible, published after The Jerusalem Bible, also is translated from the Hebrew, Greek and Aramaic.)

Before the publication of The Jerusalem Bible, all previous Catholic Bibles were translated from a translation, the Latin Vulgate. The Jerusalem Bible bypasses the Vulgate and translates directly from the original languages.

Its second unique feature is the extensive notes provided by the translators. The notes include introductory material for the different sections of the Bible, notes on the text itself, and a variety of helps, including maps and a table of weights and measures.

Value and Limitations. The value of The Jerusalem Bible, besides being an easy-to-read translation, is in its extensive notes. These are a helpful aid to better undertanding the Bible. However, it must be emphasized that this is a Catholic Bible. As such, the notes have definite leanings toward Roman Catholicism.

Although the notes are not as objectionable to Protestants as have been notes in other Catholic Bibles, they still contain teachings with which Protestants respectfully disagree. These include the Doctrine of Purgatory, the Primacy of Peter, and the Perpetual Virginity of Mary (for example, notes on 1 Corinthians 3:15, Matthew 16:19, and Matthew 1:25). Hence, in most cases Protestants will not find this translation satisfactory, although Roman Catholics would receive it wholeheartedly.

THE GOOD NEWS BIBLE

History. The background of The Good News Bible is succinctly stated in its preface:

In September 1966 the American Bible Society published The New Testament in Today's English Version, a translation intended for people everywhere for whom English is either their mother tongue or an acquired language. Shortly thereafter the United Bible Societies requested the American Bible Society to undertake on its behalf a translation of the Old Testament following the same principles.

Accordingly the American Bible Society appointed a group of translators to prepare the translation. In 1971 this group added a British consultant recommended by the British and Foreign Bible Society. The translation of the Old Testament now appears together with the fourth edition of the New Testament.

While the Old Testament was the work of several different individuals, the New Testament was the product of one man, Dr. Robert G. Bratcher. The original title to the New Testament portion was *Good News for Modern Man: The New Testament in Today's English Version*. The Good News Bible was completed in 1976.

Purpose. The idea behind the Good News Bible was to make a readable English rendition of the Bible that all English speakers could comprehend. As the preface reveals,

This translation is intended for all who use English as a means of communication; the translators have tried to avoid words and forms not in current or widespread use; but no artificial limit has been set to the range of the vocabulary employed.

Every effort has been made to use language that is natural, clear, simple and unambiguous. Consequently there has been no attempt to reproduce in English the parts of speech, sentence structure, word order, and grammatical devices of the original languages.

Unique Features. The Good News Bible, like The New English Bible, employs the concept of "dynamic equivalence" in its translation. Instead of using the usual method of translating what the author actually said, the concept of "dynamic equivalence" attempts to bring out what the author truly meant. The goal is to have the reader experience and feel the same things the original readers felt.

Another unique aspect of this work is its simplified vocabulary changing such things as "centurion" to "army officer," and "publicans" to "tax collectors."

The Good News Bible also is illustrated with line drawings that help illuminate the biblical story.

Value and Limitations. One of the great values of the Good News Bible is its ability to put the Word of God into understandable English. Those who know English as a second language will find the Good News Bible easy to follow. The simplification of technical terms also will be of great benefit to those who have no background in Christianity.

Moreover, the translation is aided by the many line drawings by Mlle. Annie Vallotton which accompany the text. The message is graphically portrayed by both the effective drawings and the clear simple English contained in the translation.

However, there are serious limitations in this work. The concept of "dynamic equivalence" is a highly questionable way of translating the Scriptures. By giving the meaning of the text rather than a translation of what it literally says, the translator goes beyond his role and becomes an interpreter.

Accuracy is sacrificed at the altar of readability, and the reader is left with the false impression that the "dynamic equivalent" rendering is what the text actually says. The idea of simplifying expressions is fine. But

sometimes they can be made too simple.
Furthermore, the Good News Bible, in its
interpretations, sometimes renders a verse
totally wrong.

A classic example is 2 Corinthians 5:21 which
reads, "Christ was without sin, but for our sake
God made Him share our sin." This statement
is in no way accurate, for God put our sins
upon Christ on the cross. He did not in any way
share sin with us.

The Good News Bible, like The Living Bible,
is a good way to introduce someone to the basic
story of the Bible. But it should not be used as
a study Bible or as a source of establishing
Bible doctrine.

NEW AMERICAN BIBLE

History. On September 30, 1943, Pope Pius XII
issued his encyclical letter concerning the
Scriptures. It read, "We ought to explain the
original text which was written by the inspired
author himself and has more authority and
greater weight than any, even the very best,
translation whether ancient or modern. This can
be done all the more easily and fruitfully if to
the knowledge of languages be joined a real
skill in literary criticism of the same text."

This set the stage for a new translation of the
Scriptures as the preface to the New American
Bible states:

Early in 1944, in conformity with the spirit of the encyclical,
and with the encouragement of Archbishop Cicognani,
Apostolic Delegate to the United States, the Bishops
Committee of the Confraternity of Christian Doctrine
requested members of the Catholic Biblical Association of
America to translate the Sacred Scriptures from the original

languages or from the oldest extant form of the text, and to present the sense of the biblical text in as correct a form as possible.

Purpose. As was the case with The Jerusalem Bible, this translation would also break with tradition and be based upon the original languages instead of on the Latin Vulgate. As the preface stated:

The first English Catholic version of the Bible, the Douay-Rheims (1582-1609/10), and its revision by Bishop Chall (1750) were based on the Latin Vulgate. In view of the relative certainties more recently attained by textual and higher criticism, it has become increasingly desirable that contemporary translations of the sacred books into English be prepared in which due reverence for the text and strict observance of the rules of criticism would be combined.

Unique Features. The New American Bible, in one sense, is the American Catholic response to the English Jerusalem Bible. It is written in American English without the British spellings and idioms contained in The Jerusalem Bible. It is not, however, a revision of The Jerusalem Bible (as the American Standard Version was of its English counterpart, the Revised Version).

It is a completely new translation, the first complete American Catholic Bible translated from the original languages. An exception to this is that the text used for translating the Psalms was not the traditional Hebrew Masoretic text but the Latin Liber Psalmorum. The footnotes reflect traditional Roman Catholic doctrine, although not as pronounced as other Catholic translations, including The Jerusalem Bible.

Value and Limitations. The value of the New American Bible is its readability for Americans. The English is clear and easy to understand. Please exercise caution in the use of this translation for two reasons. First, the notes found in the introduction to each book are liberal in tone, accepting some of the higher critical theories with regard to date and authorship of certain books. Second, although not blatant, the notes do reflect Catholic theology, aspects of which Protestants find highly questionable.

NEW ENGLISH BIBLE

History. In October 1946, delegates from a variety of church traditions—including Church of England, Church of Scotland, Congregational, and Methodist Church—resolved to undertake a new translation of the Old Testament, New Testament, and Apocrypha.

The meeting was the result of a suggestion made by the Church of Scotland at their annual meeting. In 1948, other church traditions, including the churches in Wales and Ireland, were invited to appoint representatives to the translation committee.

Purpose. The history of the Bible in English is the story of one revision after another. The translators of the New English Bible, however, felt it was time for a completely new translation. This was to be in a "timeless English," avoiding both the archaic language of yesterday and the modern slang of today.

The translation was intended to be clear to

the average person, removing any language barriers between God's Word and English-speaking people, and providing an authoritative translation suitable for public reading and worship. The translators were to take advantage of the most recent textual, linguistic and historical evidence in rendering their work.

Unique Features. The New English Bible has several striking features. The method of translation differed from the traditional. Translators always had attempted a literal word-for-word rendering of the Hebrew and Greek text into English. Instead the New English Bible attempts to provide a meaning-for-meaning rendering.

As C. H. Dodd, general director of the project, stated, "We have conceived our task to be that of understanding the original as precisely as we could (using all available aids), then saying again and again in our own native idiom what we believed the author to be saying in his" (*Introduction to the New Testament,* p. vii).

Moreover, the translators departed from the Westcott-Hort tradition in establishing their Greek text. They employed what is known as the eclectic method. That is, they were not bound to any one type of Greek text. Consequently, in several instances they incorporated questionable readings.

That the New English Bible translators did their own textual criticism is revealed in the introduction:

There is not at the present time any critical text which would command the same degree of general acceptance as the revisers' text did in its day. Nor has the time come, in the judgment of competent scholars, to construct such a text, since new material comes to light and the debate continues.

The present translators therefore could do no other than consider variant readings on their merits, and having weighed the evidence for themselves, select for translation in each passage the reading which to the best of their judgment seemed most likely to represent what the author wrote . . . (p.v).

Value and Limitations. The prime value of the New English Bible is its literary style which makes for interesting reading. The printing also is attractive. However, the limitations far outweigh the values. Attempting to reproduce a meaning-for-meaning translation usually results in a paraphrase, and that is the case with the New English Bible.

There is entirely too much interpretation as opposed to translation. Moreover, Americans, though finding the New English Bible colorful, will find the British words and expressions quite difficult. For example, 1 Corinthians 16:8 reads, "But I shall remain at Ephesus until Whitsuntide (Pentecost)."

Also, some words and expressions do not meet the intended purpose of communicating to the common people: "I broke the fangs of the miscreant" (Job 29:17). "Not for him to swill down the rivers as cream" (Job 20:17), "and they laid an information against Paul" (Acts 24:1). With its British flavor and interpretive translation, the New English Bible will not enjoy much popularity among Americans.

THE LIVING BIBLE

History. The history of The Living Bible goes back several decades to an idea conceived by Kenneth Taylor, then Director of the Moody Literature Mission of Moody Press. Being acutely aware of the need for an understandable rendition of the Bible in modern English, Taylor decided to use his commuting time on the train to and from work each day to produce a modern speech edition.

In 1962 the New Testament letters were published under the title *Living Letters.* Following this was the release of *Living Prophecies* (1965), *Living Gospels* (1966), and *Living New Testament* (1967). *Living Psalms* was also published in 1967, followed shortly thereafter by *Living Lessons of Life and Love* (1968), *Living Books of Moses* (1969) and *Living History of Israel (1970).* In 1971, the complete Living Bible was published.

Purpose. The Living Bible is not a translation but rather a paraphrase, written to communicate the thoughts of the biblical writers to modern man. This idea was expressed in the preface of the first edition of *Living Letters*:

A word should be said here about paraphrases. What are they? To paraphrase is to say something in different words than the author used.

It is a restatement of an author's thoughts, using different words than he did. This book is a paraphrase of the Old and New Testaments. Its purpose is to say as exactly as possible what the writers of the Scriptures meant, and to say it simply, expanding where necessary for a clear understanding by the modern reader.

The goal is to simplify words and expressions into a language that speaks to contemporary man. Amplification also is employed to technical terms such as "justification," "redemption" and "saints" so that the reader may more fully appreciate the meaning of each term. This was done to make the Bible more understandable, with the ultimate goal of bringing the reader into a deeper and more intimate relationship with God.

Ken Taylor was well aware of the limitations of paraphrases, as he notes in the preface of the first edition of Living Letters:

There are dangers in paraphrases, as well as values. For whenever the author's exact words are not translated from the original languages, there is a possibility that the translator, however honest, may be giving the English reader something that the original writer did not mean to say.

This is because a paraphrase is guided not only by the translator's skill in simplifying but also by the clarity of his understanding of what the author meant and by his theology. For when the Greek or Hebrew is not clear, then the theology of the translator is his guide, along with his sense of logic, unless perchance the translation is allowed to stand without any clear meaning at all. The theological lodestar in this book has been a rigid evangelical position.

Unique Features. The most unique thing about The Living Bible is that it is the most readable and understandable rendition of the biblical story available today. It is a simplified paraphrase of the Scriptures which can be understood by people of all ages and educational backgrounds.

Value and Limitations. The Living Bible has experienced tremendous circulation since its initial publication in 1971. Its great value lies in the ability to communicate the message of the Bible in an understandable fashion. It is an excellent way to introduce someone to the story of the Bible.

There are, however, factors regarding The Living Bible which readers need to be aware of. For one thing, it is not a word-for-word translation but a paraphrase or commentary. Consequently, the reader should avoid drawing theological or doctrinal conclusions based on a paraphrase without additionally consulting and comparing the original texts or a word-for-word translation.

Still, The Living Bible is probably the best way to introduce someone to the biblical story.

NEW AMERICAN STANDARD BIBLE

History. The New American Standard Bible resulted from the determination to revise the American Standard Version of 1901. It is the work of the Lockman Foundation, a nonprofit Christian corporation formed in 1942 to promote, among other things, translations of the Bible.

The Foundation already had produced the Amplified Bible (completed 1965). It produced the Gospel of John in 1960 and continued until the entire Bible was completed in 1971.

Purpose. The New American Standard Bible was produced to acquaint the public with the virtues of the American Standard Version of 1901, as the translators state in their preface:

Perhaps the most weighty impetus for this undertaking can be attributed to a disturbing awareness that the American

Standard Version of 1901 was fast disappearing from the scene.

As a generation "which knew not Joseph" was born, even so a generation unacquainted with this great and important work has come into being. Recognizing a responsibility to posterity, the Lockman Foundation felt an urgency to rescue this noble achievement from an inevitable demise, to preserve it as a heritage for coming generations, and to do so in such a form as the demands of passing time dictate.

Although the Revised Standard Version, like the New American Standard Bible, revises the American Standard Version of 1901, the translators of the New American Standard Bible seem to have felt less than satisfied with some of the anomalies of the Revised Standard Version.

So the translators of the New American Standard Bible attempted to bring the American Standard Version up to date, to be as faithful to the original languages as possible, and to present a clear and readable style based upon current usage.

Unique Features. The translators of the New American Standard Bible paid special attention in their rendering of the Greek tenses (making careful distinction in English, for example, between the Greek aorist tense and the Greek imperfect tense) in order to clarify the meaning of the writer.

Also, the New American Standard Bible retains the familiar "Thou," "Thee" and "Thy" forms of the personal pronoun only in reference to Deity, replacing these archaic forms with the modern "you" and "your" when referring to those besides God. The divine name was rendered Lord, as in the King James Version, discarding the 1901 American Standard Version "Jehovah."

Value and Limitations. With the helpful cross-reference system, and the painstaking efforts made by the translators to bring out the distinction between the Greek tenses, the New American Standard Bible is an excellent study tool for the serious student of Scripture. Although it is not as readable as some translations, its accuracy is second to none. If one desires to study the Scripture, the New American Standard Bible is perhaps the best Bible available.

NEW INTERNATIONAL VERSION

History. The preface to the New International Version reveals the background to this newest of the modern translations:

The New International Version is a completely new translation of the Holy Bible made by over a hundred scholars working directly from the best available Hebrew, Aramaic and Greek texts. It had its beginning in 1965 when, after several years of exploratory study by committees from the Christian Reformed Church and the National Association of Evangelicals, a group of scholars met at Palos Heights, Illinois, and concurred in the need for a new translation of the Bible in contemporary English. This group, though not made up of official church representatives, was transdenominational. Its conclusion was endorsed by a large number of leaders from many denominations who met in Chicago in 1966.

Purpose. As the translators state in the preface, the goals for the New International Version were an accurate and clear translation of the

Scriptures, "suitable for public and private reading, teaching, preaching, memorizing and liturgical use."

Another goal of the translators was to present the thought and meaning of the biblical writers rather than to simply present a word-for-word translation. The language would omit the archaisms found in other translations such as the traditional pronouns "Thou," "Thee," and "Thine" used in referring to God. Their intended result was a modern-speech translation that would be faithful to the meaning of the Scriptures inasmuch as each translator shared the conviction that the Bible was the authoritative and infallible Word of God.

Unique Features. The New International Version is the most recent of all modern speech translations. Moreover it is, as its title indicates, international in its composition, being the work of scholars from America, England, Canada, Australia and New Zealand. These scholars represented many denominations: Anglican, Assemblies of God, Brethren, Lutheran, Nazarene, Presbyterian, and a number of others. This was to safeguard against incorporating the traditions of any one denomination.

Value and Limitations. The value of the New International Version can be found in its readability. The goal of the translators for clarity and literary quality has been accomplished.

The New International Version, however, is not without problems. This translation is an attempt to bring out the thoughts and meanings of the biblical writers. When this is attempted, the possibility of paraphrasing becomes great. In too many instances, the New International Version is guilty of trying to get across the meaning of the author rather than directly translating what the writer said. When this is done the reader is locked into the meaning provided by the translators (which may be the correct meaning, but also may be an incorrect one).

The reader, moreover, has no way of knowing what is merely the translator's interpretation and naturally assumes everything to be part of the sacred text. While some degree of interpretation is necessary, the job of translators is not to use the text to tell the reader what is meant. Margins or footnotes are better suited for such commentary. The text should be a translation of what the writer says.

Even difficult expressions are to be translated accordingly, or the product becomes a commentary instead of a translation. Some readability may be sacrificed in avoiding paraphrasing, yet accuracy should always take precedence over readability.

The task of translating the Bible is not easy, and in spite of the problems mentioned above, the New International Version will continue as a popular and readable translation.

Is there a supernatural character to the Bible?

The Bible is more than an ordinary book. It reveals itself to be the supernatural Word of God written through human beings. The Bible is the Word of God written in the words of men. This is possible because the God of the Bible is limitless in His ability. We are driven to this conclusion, not because of any preconceived biased or circular reasoning but because of the evidence.

To be considered to have come from an all-powerful God, a book must meet certain requirements. First it must be transmitted to us accurately from the time it was originally written so that we may have an exact representation of what God said and did. Also, it must be correct when it deals with historical personages and events. A book that confuses names, dates and events has no right to claim it comes from an infallible God. Furthermore, any revelation from God should be without any scientific absurdities which would betray mere human authorship.

At the very least, any work coming from God must meet the above requirements. The Bible does this and so much more. When the facts are considered, the Bible reveals a divine origin.

The text of the Bible has been transmitted accurately. We may rest assured that what we have today is a correct representation of what was originally given. For example, there is more evidence for the reliability of the text of the New Testament as an accurate reflection of what was initially written than there is for any thirty pieces of classical literature put together.

If one will judge the New Testament documents with the same standards or tests applied to any one of the Greek classics, the evidence overwhelmingly favors the New Testament. If a person contends that we have a reliable text of the classics, then he would be forced to admit we have a reliable text of the New Testament.

Not only does the New Testament text have far superior evidence for reliability than the classics, it also is in better shape textually than the thirty-seven plays of William Shakespeare written in the seventeenth century after the invention of printing. In every one of Shakespeare's plays there are lacunae (gaps) in the printed text where we have no idea what originally was said. This forces textual scholars to make a conjectural emendation (a fancy term for "good guess") to fill in the blank. With the abundance of manuscripts (handwritten copies) of the New Testament (over 25,000), nothing has been lost through the transmission of the text.

The history recorded in the Scriptures also proves to be accurate. As far as we have been able to check them out, the names, places and events mentioned in the Bible have been recorded accurately.

For example, the book of Acts, once considered spurious, has been vindicated by modern discoveries. As the Roman historian A. N. Sherwin-White says, "For Acts the confirmation of historicity is overwhelming . . . any attempt to reject its basic historicity even in matters of detail must now appear absurd. Roman historians have long taken it for granted" (A. M. Sherwin-White, *Roman Society and Roman Law in the New Testament*, p. 189).

Those who contend that the Bible is unreliable historically are not professional historians. This is the reason the great archaeologist William F. Albright said, "All radical schools in New Testament criticism which have existed in the past or which exist today are pre-archaeological, and are, therefore, since they were built 'in der Luft' (in the air), quite antiquated today" (William F. Albright, "Retrospect and Prospect in New Testament Archaeology," in *The Teacher's Yoke,* E. Jerry Vardaman, ed., p. 29). The testimony of the historical evidence is that the Bible can be trusted as an accurate document.

Where the Bible speaks on matters of science, it does so with simple yet correct terms devoid of absurdities. Where non-biblical accounts of the formation of the universe and other scientific matters border on the ridiculous, the Scriptures nowhere are guilty of this. It is not what could be expected from a book written by men during pre-scientific times.

Matters dealing with science also are written with restraint (such as the Genesis account of creation). The biblical narrative is accurate and concise in direct contrast to the crude Babylonian story which contends the earth was made from a dismembered part of one of the gods after in-fighting in heaven.

Likewise, the flood of Noah's day is given in simple but accurate terms which are sensible scientifically. (See *The Genesis Flood,* by John C. Whitcomb and Henry Morris, regarding such matters as the seaworthiness of the ark, etc.)

The clarity and restraint which the Bible shows toward the scientific is exactly what we should expect if this book were inspired by God.

Not only does the Bible meet the minimum requirements for being a book coming from God, it also contains powerful evidence of having a divine origin.

This can be illustrated by the magnificent unity of the Scriptures. When the implications are considered, the unity of the Bible gives us a reason for believing it to be a supernatural book.

Consider this: If you selected ten people living at the same time in history, living in the same basic geographical area, with the same basic educational background, speaking the same language, and you asked them to write independently on their conception of God, the result would be anything but a united testimony.

It would not help if you asked them to write about man, woman or human suffering, for it is the nature of human beings to differ on controversial subjects. However, the biblical writers not only agree on these subjects but on dozens more. They have complete unity and harmony. There is only one story in the Scriptures from beginning to end, although God used different human authors to record it. The supernatural character of the Bible is one reason we believe Christianity to be true.

Is Noah's Ark still on Mt. Ararat?

One of the great mysteries of the twentieth century surrounds the survival of the ancient ark of Noah. The Bible says a great flood transpired approximately 5,000 years ago in which Noah and his family survived by means of a large wooden vessel which they had constructed. This ship eventually came to rest upon the mountains of Ararat (Genesis 8:4).

If the flood account is true, what happened to the ark? Could it be possible that it has survived to this day? If so, what is the evidence for its existence?

We have, for years, followed the expeditions to Mt. Ararat to attempt recovery of the ark. We are constantly asked our opinion of the matter, so we felt it necessary to put the issue in perspective. We are not saying anything that has not already been said concerning the evidence for the ark's existence. But we are attempting to give a summary of what has happened and the way things now stand. It's a fascinating story that everyone in our modern world should be made aware of.

BIBLICAL SETTING

"Then the Lord saw that the wickedness of man was great on the earth, and that every intent of the thoughts of his heart was only evil continually. And the Lord was sorry that He had made man on the earth, and He was grieved in His heart. And the Lord said, 'I will blot out the man whom I have created from the face of the land, from man to animals to creeping things and to birds of the sky; for I am sorry that I have made them.' But Noah found favor in the eyes of the Lord" (Genesis 6:5-8).

The earth, filled with violence and corruption, was ripe for judgment by God almighty. Consequently, God decided to destroy those living on the earth with a great flood. However, righteous Noah and his family would be spared from this deluge by means of a large wooden vessel God commanded them to build. "Then God said to Noah . . . make for yourself an ark of gopher wood; you shall make the ark with rooms, and shall cover it inside and out with pitch. And this is how you shall make it: The length of the ark three hundred cubits, its breadth fifty cubits, and its height thirty cubits. You shall make a window for the ark, and finish it to a cubit from the top; and set the door of the ark in the side of it; you shall make it with lower, second, and third decks" (Genesis 6:13-16).

Having received the specifications of the ship, Noah and his family spent 120 years constructing the ark. Eventually, the promised flood came, destroying all life except Noah and his family and two of each animal that were brought to the ark. "And the water prevailed more and more upon the earth, so that all the high mountains everywhere under the heavens were covered. The water prevailed fifteen cubits higher, and the mountains were covered. And all flesh that moved on the earth perished" (Genesis 7:19-21).

Finally the rain stopped "and the water receded steadily from the earth, and at the end of one hundred and fifty days the water decreased. And in the seventh month, on the seventeenth day of the month, the ark rested

upon the mountains of Ararat" (Genesis 8:3, 4).
The Fact of the Flood. The verification of the
Genesis flood is given by no less a figure than
Jesus Christ who compared the flood to His
second coming: "For the coming of the Son of
Man will be just like the days of Noah. For as
in those days which were before the flood they
were eating and drinking, they were marrying
and giving in marriage, until the day that Noah
entered the ark" (Matthew 24:37-38). The fact
of the flood is assumed by Jesus. This settles the
issue for the believer. If Jesus is the one whom
He made Himself out to be, God in human
flesh, then whenever He speaks on a matter He
does so with final authority. Since He verified
the occurrence of the flood, the issue is forever
settled.

The Ark. The ark which God commanded Noah
to build was three hundred cubits long, fifty
cubits wide, and thirty cubits high. A cubit
equals approximately 18 inches, making the ark
450 feet long, 75 feet wide, and 45 feet high. Its
total capacity would be 1,518,750 cubit feet. On
its ability to hold all the animals see our work,
Answers.

Its Seaworthiness. Was the ark capable of
withstanding the violent force which the flood
would place upon it? Dr. Henry Morris, former
professor of hydraulic engineering and chairman
of the department of civil engineering at
Virginia Polytechnical Institute, has shown that
the size and design of the ark would have made
it stable, able to withstand the onslaught of the
flood ("The Ark of Noah," Creation Research
Society Quarterly, VIII, 1971, pp. 142-144).

Morris' conclusion: "In every way, therefore, the ark as designed was highly stable, admirably suited for its purpose of riding out the storms of the year of the great flood."

British scientist Frederick A. Filby also comments on its seaworthiness:

The Babylonian account which speaks of the ark as a cube betrays complete ignorance. Such a vessel would spin slowly around. But the biblical ratios leave nothing to be desired. These ratios are important from the point of view of stability, of pitching and of rolling. The ratio of length to breadth, 300 to 50, is 6 to 1. Taking the mean of six present-day ships of approximately the same size, selected from six different shipping lines, we obtain, as an example, a ratio of 8.1 to 1. The giant liner *Queen Elizabeth* has a ratio 8.16 to 1, while the *Canberra* has 8.2 to 1. But these vessels were designed for speed; the ark was not. Some of the giant tankers have ratios around 7 to 1. Still more interesting are the figures for the *Great Britain*, designed by I. K. Brunel in 1844. Her dimensions were 322 feet by 51 feet by 32 1/2 feet, so that the ratios are almost exactly those of the ark. Brunel had the accumulated knowledge of generations of shipbuilders to draw upon. The ark was the first of its kind! (*The Flood Reconsidered*, p. 93).

Its Construction. The question also is raised as to the possibility of ancient man constructing such a large vessel. Was it too large an undertaking for someone living in Noah's day? Filby gives a resounding answer:

It seems reasonable, on the natural level, to suppose that Noah possessed that constructive genius which manifests itself from time to time throughout history in the construction of something far beyond the achievement of a man's contemporaries.

It was surely the type of genius shown by Imhotep in the design of the Step Pyramid, by the architect of the Hanging

Gardens of Babylon, by Ictinus and Callicrates in the building of the Parthenon, and by Chares of Lindus in the construction of Colossus of Rhodes.

If we reject the story, and say that the task was too great, and that no man could have stood out so far ahead of his contemporaries, then, we must reject the other seven wonders of the ancient world. Noah was only the first of that line of geniuses who designed and constructed something which far outshone the capacity of their contemporaries (Frederick A. Filby, *The Flood Reconsidered,* Zondervan Publishing Company, 1971, p. 80).

Therefore, there is no need to appeal to the miraculous with regard to the construction of the ark. Ancient history affords us many examples of amazing construction of unbelievable proportions.

Mt. Ararat. One of the most graphic descriptions of the Ararat regions was given by M. M. Kalisch in his commentary on Genesis written more than 100 years ago,

Ararat consists of two unequal peaks, both of which disappear in the clouds; the loftier summit is 16,254 Parisian feet high, while the other northwestern pinnacle rises to the elevation of 12,284 Parisian feet above the level of the sea. Both are 12,000 yards distance from each other. . . .

The plateau on which Ararat rises is of considerable height. But, viewed from the vast plain which skirts its base, it appears as if the hugest mountains of the world had been piled upon each other to form this one sublime immensity of earth, and rock, and snow. . . .

These two peaks of Ararat are separated by a wild and dark chasm, cutting deeply into the interior of the mountain, filling the spectator with horror and shuddering, and containing in its innermost recesses immense masses of never melting ice of the dimensions of enormous towers. And this stupendous and fearful abyss is probably the exhausted crater of Ararat, become wider than ever since the eruption of 1840, and since that catastrophe, exposing on its upper sides the white, yellow, and vitreous feldspars of which the mountain consists. Pious hermits seem, in that fearful precipice, to have sought refuge from the cares and vanities of the world. . . .

The vegetation on the sides of the mountain is extremely scanty; stones, sand, and lava form their mass. Eagles and hawks soar around its majestic summits. In the hottest season only, the snow melts on the peak of the Little Ararat; and this event is used as a kind of calendar by the agriculturalists in the surrounding villages. In September and October it is generally free of its hoary crust. But the Great Ararat is, for about three miles from the summit, covered with eternal snow and ice, and for the greater part of the year gloomily shrouded in dense and heavy cloud. The summit of this noble mountain forms a slightly convex, almost circular platform, about two hundred pace in circuit. . . .

At the margin, the summit slopes off precipitously, especially on the northeastern side. A gentle depression connects this pinnacle with the somewhat lower eminence at a distance of 397 yards. Here it is believed the ark of Noah rested. (M. M. Kalisch, *Historical and Critical Commentary on the Old Testament: Genesis,* London: Longman Green, 1858).

HISTORICAL INQUIRY

The Book of Genesis clearly states that the ark of Noah landed on Mt. Ararat. From ancient times until today there have been accounts of the ark's sighting on Mt. Ararat.

Fernand Navarra, in his book, *Noah's Ark: I Touched It* (pp. 1-3), has these fascinating comments:

The earliest known witness to the continued presence of Noah's ark on Mount Ararat was Berose, or Berosus, a Chaldean priest who wrote histories of Chaldea and Assyria.

This ancient stated that in his time (circa 475 B.C., almost 2,000 years after the traditional date of the great flood) people still ascended the mountain and scraped the bituminous coating from the wood of the ark. They used the pieces of bitumen as talismans.

Josephus, who lived during the latter part of the first century, wrote in his *Antiquities of the Jews* that the Armenians call the place where Noah landed "The Place of Descent; for the ark being saved in that place, its remains are shown there by the inhabitants to this day."

Josephus cites other witnesses: "Hieronymus the Egyptian, who wrote the Phoenician Antiquities, and Mnaseas, and a great many more, also make mention of the same. Nay, Nicolaus of Damascus, in his ninety-sixth book, hath a particular relation about them, where he speaks thus: 'There is a great mountain in Armenia, over Minyas, called Baris, upon which it is reported that many who fled at the time of the Deluge were saved; and that one who was carried in an ark came on shore upon the top of it; and that the remains of the timber were a great while preserved.' St. Theophilus of Antioch confirmed this statement."

In A.D. 330, Jacob, a patriarch of Nisbis, attempted to reach the top. He failed, but according to a legend an angel visited him and gave him a fragment of the Ark. This fragment was reportedly kept in the church of Etchmiadzin, near Ararat, until the building was destroyed by the earthquake of 1829 and the fragment was lost.

William of Ruysbroeck, a Flemish traveler of the thirteenth century, journeyed near the foot of Mount Ararat in 1254 on his way back from an expedition to the Karakoram Range. He wrote that the mountain, which he called "Masis," was "the mother of the world," and that was why nobody could reach the top. *"Super Masis nullus debet ascendere, quia est mater mundi."* This myth of Ararat's inaccessibility circulated for centuries.

Marco Polo (ca. 1254-1324) mentioned the existence of the ark and described Mount Ararat as a huge mountain, around which one could not travel in less than two days, and whose summit could not be reached because of everlasting snow.

Sir John Maundeville told the story of Jacob of Nisbis, with one variation. The angel did not give the patriarch a fragment of the ark, but he helped him climb up the mountain. Jacob himself found and brought back the fragment which was worshiped later in Etchmiadzin. According to Maundeville, many natives boasted that they had seen and touched the Ark, but he remained skeptical. "No one has gone to the top of Mount Ararat since the monk Jacob. It is impossible to believe those who claim that they have made the ascent."

Jean Chardin, a seventeenth-century French traveler, mentioned the same miracle story in his *Voyage to Persia and the East Indies*. Chardin seems to have believed the story, marveling that the monk could climb up Mount Ararat, "when in all seasons of the year the mountain is one enormous mass of snow."

In the eighteenth century, Joseph Pitton de Tournefort, a botanist from Aix, France, collected plants on the slopes of Mount Ararat, but he climbed no higher than the second third of the mountain. Some time later, James J. Morier (died 1849), British diplomat and novelist, failed in an attempt to scale the mountain. A pasha from the Turkish town of Bayazid, located at the foot of Ararat, also failed. He had left on horse back with a numerous escort, but had to stop far below the snow zone. When a late eighteenth-century Persian shah offered a large sum of money to the first person who would reach the summit, nobody even attempted to climb.

In 1800 an American, Claudius James Rich, related the unverifiable claims of a certain Aga Hussein, who claimed to have reached the top of the mountain and seen the remains of the ark.

The history of ascent of Mount Ararat in modern times begins in 1829, with a Russian, Frederic Parrot.

Parrot was a doctor, a professor at Dorpat University, Estonia, and one of the first alpinists.

John Warwick Montgomery, in *The Quest for Noah's Ark* (pp. 314-317), adds other details regarding sightings of the ark:

Even in the face of powerful archeological attestations as to the historicity of the first five books of the Bible—even though Moses' writings have proved themselves historically in accord with Jesus' own valuation of them—popular opinion still regards the opening portion of the book of Genesis as religious myth. Prior to Abraham, biblical material remains suspect. In particular, the Genesis account of Noah and the Ark (Genesis 6-9) seems to many to be the archetypal children's story.

Yet one should pause a moment before embracing this commonly held viewpoint. Granted, archeological confirmation of biblical material has not gone much farther back than Abraham (Genesis 11)—but a century ago, as we have seen, Abraham was confidently regarded as myth! From Genesis 11 to Genesis 9 is a very short distance, and scientific biblical archeology has been closing gaps like this steadily for a century. Ought we not perhaps learn from experience?

Moreover, traditions of a universal Flood are worldwide, among peoples as diverse as Laplandeers and Fiji islanders, and these traditions very often make mention of a boat by which a few escaped the destructive waters. My interest as a historian in ancient Flood accounts led me to investigate all the documentary records of the actual survival of Noah's vessel, which, according to the book of Genesis, landed "upon the mountains of Ararat" (8:4). The extra-biblical reports commence with the historical Berossus (third century B.C.), who states that "of this ship that grounded in Armenia some part still remains in the mountains" and that people removed pitch from it to use for amulets. From Berossus to the twentieth century there is a steady stream of such report of the ark's survival, almost invariably associated with Greater Ararat (Mount Agri) on the eastern border of present-day Turkey.

Among the most recent testimonies are the following:

Testimony of the Ark's Survival	Source of the Testimony
i. Personally seen and climbed upon by a youthful Armenian (1902).	Interview with the Armenian (tape recorded).

THE BIBLE 81 ∎

ii. Seen at close hand by a White Russian military patrol (1916–17).	Interviews with members of the families of now-deceased soldiers on the patrol and with officers who knew them (sworn statements).
iii. Explorer Hardwicke Knight comes upon a rectangular wooden framework in the ice on Ararat (1930s).	Knight's sworn statement.
iv. A boat-like form protruding from the ice on Ararat is photographed by engineer George Jefferson Greene from a helicopter (1952).	Drawing by a fellow engineer made on the basis of the deceased Greene's no longer extant photographs.
v. French amateur explorer Fernand Navarra sees under glacial ice on Ararat a boat-shaped form of the biblical dimensions of the ark (1952), and later (1955) succeeded in obtaining some of its wood, which definitely is handtooled, apparently pitch-(bitumen-) impregnated, and at least 5,000 years old.	Navarra's accounts in his two books (*L'Expedition au Mont Ararat; J'al trouve l'Arche de Noe*); personal interview with him and examination of the wood; wood analysis reports from the Forestry Institute of Research and Experimentation, Madrid, Spain, and from the Prehistory Institute of the University of Bordeaux's Faculty of Sciences.

Montgomery continues:

Because of the powerful nature of this circumstantial evidence, I myself have gone to Mount Ararat four times (August, 1970, 1971, and 1972; April, 1973), ascending to the peak of this exceedingly high (5,165m./16,946 ft.) and treacherous peak on August 17, 1970. Ararat overlooks the

Turkish-Russian border and is in a region controlled by the Turkish military; it has therefore been impossible, sad to say, to obtain government permissions to carry out the kind of extensive on-site research required to confirm past testimonies and bring about a firm discovery.

On returning from Turkey to the United States in September of this last year (1973), however, I was contacted by Mr. Thomas B. Turner of McDonnell Douglas Astronautics Company, who had been in touch with M. Delaney of the Earth Resources Observation Satellite Center, Sioux Falls, South Dakota, where ERTS data are stored. While checking ERTS imagery of the Ararat region, Delaney had found a peculiar rectangular shape, apparently foreign to the mountain. Most remarkable was the location of the rectangle: in the very quandrant of the mountain where previous ground sightings had concentrated. Delaney had not known this when he located the strange shape; indeed, he did not read my book collecting past sightings until introduced to it by Turner.

True, the ERTS data are by no means definitive. The overall rectangle is larger than the dimensions of the biblical Ark (there is a smaller, perceptibly whiter area within the total rectangle, but the resolution capabilities of the imagery do not permit determining its size). Jerald Cook's staff at the Center for Remote Sensing of the Environmental Research Institute of Michigan has subjected the imagery to careful scouting and is unable to pronounce upon it with certainty.

But are not the possibilities breathtaking? As Belon and Miller rightly observe: "Satellite remote sensing of the environment must be coupled with data acquired from aircraft as well as with surface observations in order to be completely effective." The use of aircraft in the Ararat region is out of the question because of the military situation, and we have just received word from Ankara that—doubtless because of the native Kurdish uprisings in Iraq and Iran near Ararat and the Turkish border—no insite exploration of Ararat will be permitted this coming summer. [Roger-X. Lanteri, "Kurdes: l'ultimatum," *L'Express* (March 25-31, 1974), pp. 62, 63.]

CIRCUMSTANTIAL EVIDENCE

Certain facts in the investigation of Noah's ark
are beyond all dispute. These include:

1. At about the 14,000 foot level on Mt. Ararat in
   Turkey, there is a very large wooden boat-like
   structure buried beneath many feet of ice and
   snow.

2. A boat-like structure has been mentioned as
   being on Mt. Ararat by explorers and historians
   of several civilizations beginning as early as
   700 B.C.

3. During the 1800s, this structure was observed by
   many local explorers including numerous Turkish
   military authorities who gave the structure offici
   governmental recognition in the news media.

4. In 1955, a filmed expedition recovered wood fro
   the structure nearly thirty-five feet below the
   surface of an ice pack.

5. The recovered wood, subjected to numerous typ
   of dating tests revealed an age range of from 1,2
   to 5,000 years old.

6. Early in the decade of the '70s, American spy
   planes, and weather and military satellites
   photographed the structure on Mt. Ararat.

7. The only specific historical source that can be us
   to identify this artifact is the biblical book of
   Genesis which mentions the ancient landing of a
   large boat "on the mountains of Ararat." (From
   Dave Balsiger and Charles E. Sellier, Jr., *In
   Search of Noah's Ark,* p. 2.)

When one considers the above facts, a good
case can be made on circumstantial grounds, for
the ark's existence. Though by no means
conclusive, the evidence is highly significant.
The fact remains that something is up there.
And whatever that something may be, it is

thousands of years old, large, wooden, and hand-tooled. If it is not Noah's ark, what then is it? This question must be addressed.

ITS SIGNIFICANCE IF REAL

If it can be verified beyond a shadow of a doubt that Noah's ark is indeed still surviving on Mt. Ararat, the significance of such a verification would be monumental. The recovery of the ark would strongly suggest that the great flood did occur. How else, one might ask, could the ark have reached such a height? There are not any trees in the immediate vicinity with which to construct the ark, so some theory must be postulated as to how it got there.

If no rational explanation can be given to justify its existence, then the biblical explanation, being supernatural, must be seriously considered. The Bible's account of the flood and the ark would receive strong confirmation. If this can be confirmed, then it indirectly demonstrates the existence of God, for the idea of an ark assumes a flood which, in turn, assumes a judgment. It is not feasible to suppose this massive ship just happened to be around when the rains came and its inhabitants climbed in and survived for an extended period of time. The Bible specifically says that the ark was constructed to preserve Noah, his family, and two of each animal from the flood's destruction, which was a judgment from God. Based upon this line of argumentation, a case can be made from the ark data for the existence of God. This argument, while based on circumstantial evidence, cannot easily be dismissed.

Several objections exist in identifying the structure on Mt. Ararat as Noah's ark.

The Site of the Landing. It never has been firmly established that the mountain of the present day expeditions is the one on which Noah's ark landed. Arthur Custance, researcher, points this out: "Moreover, there is no certainty, as has been pointed out time and again, that the ark landed on this mountain. The Scriptures say only that it landed on the mountains (plural) of Ararat (Genesis 8:4), Ararat being almost certainly a *district* (Jeremiah 51:27) containing more than one potential landing site. (Arthur C. Custance, *The Flood: Local or Global,* p. 104.)

However, the explorations have taken place on Greater Ararat, the largest mountain in the region, which has a long-standing tradition as being the place where the ark came to rest. Greater Ararat is the most likely candidate, considering its height and the long and well-documented tradition concerning the survival of the structure. Also, all the sightings and the wooden fragments found have been from Greater Ararat. Hence Custance's argument here is not particularly persuasive.

Many Legends. Another objection along a similar line comes from Bernard Ramm who says, "Legends of finding the ark of Mt. Ararat have flourished for centuries. . . . To date, all such legends of finding the ark are fictions. As we shall subsequently indicate, the ark did not come down on the top of Mt. Ararat (some 17,000 feet high), but on the Ararat range. If that is the case, the ark disappeared a long time ago through rot, or for firewood, or for building material" (Bernard Ramm, *The Christian View of Science and Scripture,* p. 158).

Too High? The 17,000-foot height where the ark now allegedly sits presents a difficulty for some writers: "The waters carried the ark up to the Ararat range. The Hebrew text does not mean the ark was deposited on the 1,000-foot summit of the peak, but that the ark rested somewhere on the Ararat range. It would have taken a special miracle to get Noah and his family down from such dizzy mountain heights where the cold would have been extreme" (Bernard Ramm, *The Christian View of Science and Scripture,* p. 162).

Custance argues in a similar vein:

In all the present sightings, either aircraft spottings or binoculars or mountain climbing has been involved, suggesting that the site of land was, or is now, difficult to reach. Many of the animals would have trouble descending to sea level. . . .

The scenario we thus create may be quite unrealistic. Until we know with greater certainty what the phrase "the mountains of Ararat" actually signified to the writer, we are not in a good position to assert vigorously that the ark landed at the elevation of several thousand feet on what is now known as Mount Ararat.

The stories reported by early writers, like Josephus (*Antiquities,* I,iii,5), of wood taken from the ark the first few centuries of the present era almost certainly exclude any supposed site such as is currently in question, the visiting of which means the mounting of an alpine expedition with all the sophistication of modern mountain-climbing equipment (Arthur C. Custance, *The Flood: Local or Global,* p. 105).

However, the Bible makes it clear that the ark did land high atop Mt. Ararat as Arthur Whitcomb shows:

One hundred and fifty days after the flood began, the waters started to subside and the ark grounded on one of the highest mountain peaks (for the ark grounded on the very same day the waters began to assuage—Genesis 7:11; 8:3-4). However, *ten weeks* later, nothing could be seen above the water level except other mountain peaks (8:4-5)! And still another *twenty-one* weeks were required for the waters to subside sufficiently for Noah to disembark safely *in the mountains of Ararat!* How a flood of such depth and duration could have covered only a limited portion of the earth's surface has never been satisfactorily explained" (John C. Whitcomb, *The World That Perished*, p. 46).

Where did it land? Custance presents another interesting objection:

Almost every search has been directed toward the side, rather than the top, of the supposed site of landing. This seems difficult to justify unless one supposes that after settling at the top and unloading, the ark later slipped down the side. Is it likely that such a huge vessel would be so easily shifted—unless by an earthquake or a landslide? But the assumption always seems to be that this, the present supposed site, is where it *landed*. Then one must ask, How did it land well down the mountainside without the dry land having already appeared? If it had settled, let us say, 1,000 feet from the top, would not the 1,000 feet of exposed land from which the waters must have already declined have constituted "dry land" long before the ark touched down? How then can the ark be said to have bottomed some 74 days *before* dry land was anywhere visible?

The olive leaf brought back to the ark by the dove seems to suggest that the bird had found green trees at some elevation which must have been far below the elevation at which the ark is *reportedly* resting today. And if my argument has any force regarding the nonappearance of dry land when the ark settled, the ark must have landed at an elevation even higher than this. In that case, where could a dove possibly find an olive leaf at such a high elevation? Most of the land around was still under water. It was, moreover, an olive leaf "plucked off" (Genesis 8:11), i.e., not a bit of flotsam and jetsam but a leaf from a living tree. It may have been found some distance perhaps from the ark, but it seems reasonable to suppose that the ark was, in fact, not resting at an altitude of several thousand feet, and thus the olive tree had not been submerged under these thousands of feet of water: possibly it had been an olive tree on the crown of a rise of land like the Mount of Olives, and scarcely submerged at all" (Arthur Custance, *The Flood: Local or Global,* pp. 104-105).

This objection is not really difficult to deal with. It is not necessary at all to assume that the present site of the remains of the ark is where it landed. There is good evidence to believe that in recent times the ark has slidden somewhat downward (see John Warwick Montgomery, *The Quest for Noah's Ark,* 2d ed., p. 374).

A Sign of Christ's Second Coming? Many questions have arisen concerning the timing of the discovery of Noah's ark. Why does it seem so near? If found, what will it mean to the skeptical age in which we live? One very thought-provoking possibility is that God will use it as a sign to indicate the soon return of Christ, remembering Jesus Himself said the time of his return would be likened to the days of Noah. John Warwick Montgomery develops this thought:

Will there be "earthly things" provided as specific signs and warnings of the end of the age? Jesus' answer is yes, for Matthew 24 and its parallels tell us of natural calamities, wars, etc. that will precede His return. Could an even more explicit sign be in preparation for a world that has largely forgotten the days of Noah and cares little for anything but "eating and drinking, marrying and giving in marriage"? Is it possible that God has reserved the very vessel that, like the wooden Cross, saved those who entrusted themselves to it, so as to bring it forth as a most concrete indicator of the return of the days of Noah? Such a sign would no more force the conversion of those who prefer their values to

God's values than the manifest miracles of Christ convinced
the men of His time who would not subject their lives to
Him. But to deny Him they had to resort to such absurdities
as "He casts out devils by the prince of devils"; and the
weight of evidence for God's truth has pushed unbelievers
to comparable irrationality in every age. Might the God of
all grace—who, as in the case of doubting Thomas, so often
goes the second mile in offering His truth to the
undeserving—not present one final confirmation of His
Word to those who "hearing can still hear" before He
brings down the curtain on human history?

The Bible does not require an affirmative answer to this
question, but such an answer would be entirely consistent
with the divine operations as recorded in Holy Writ (John
Warwick Montgomery, *The Quest for Noah's Ark,* rev. ed.,
pp. 287,288).

A PRECAUTION AS A BASIS FOR BELIEF

There is good circumstantial evidence that part
of Noah's ark continues to survive on Mt.
Ararat. And it is conceivable that someday it
will be unearthed with its true identity being
exposed. While the prospects are indeed
exciting, a word of warning needs to be given.
The truthfulness of the Christian faith does not
rest upon vindicating the existence of Noah's
ark on Mt. Ararat. Suppose, for example, that
it is demonstrated that the large wooden object
on Ararat is not Noah's ark. What would
Christianity have lost? The answer is nothing.

Our Christian faith is built upon the fact that
Jesus of Nazareth, once and for all,
demonstrated Himself to be the unique Son of
God by His sinless life, miracles, and
resurrection from the dead. Christianity stands
or falls on the person of Jesus Christ. If He can
be refuted, then the Christian faith also can be
refuted. However, alleged artifacts such as the

ark of Noah or the shroud of Turin, whether they be factual or not, do not constitute a basis for faith. Their authenticity, even if it can be established, will not necessarily create belief.

The Bible affords two examples that are appropriate in dealing with artifacts. In the book of Numbers, God sent serpents to judge His rebellious people, whereupon the people called to Him for deliverance. God then instructed Moses to erect a bronze serpent in the center of the camp as an object of faith. Those who were bitten by the deadly serpents could look to the serpent in faith and live. However, this same bronze serpent was discovered several hundred years later by the Jews in their temple.

Their response was to worship this object. They missed the whole point. The bronze serpent was not anything holy in itself; it was to direct one's faith to God. The ark also should serve in this capacity; it should not be venerated.

Jesus gave us an important lesson in His account of the rich man in hell. The man had five brothers whom he desired to warn against the fate for which they were headed. He wanted someone to return from the dead and warn them, for he thought they surely would believe such a person. However, he was scolded for this misconception. "If they hear not Moses and the prophets," Jesus said, "neither will they be persuaded, though one rose from the dead" (Luke 16:19-31). In other words, if they will not believe the overwhelming evidence already given them, they certainly will not be convinced by any further evidence. Why? Because their problem was not an intellectual or evidential one. Enough evidence exists for anyone to make an intelligent decision for Jesus Christ, but no amount of evidence will force someone to believe against his will. The verifying of Noah's ark will substantiate the faith of believers but will not necessarily create faith in unbelievers who are unwilling to come to terms with their spiritual needs.

Present State of the Search. The strained relationship between the United States and the Turkish government, along with the ever-increasing strategic location of Ararat (twenty miles from the Russian border) have kept recent expeditions to a minimum. No significant discoveries have been made in the last few years.

Conclusion. The history of the sightings, along with the hand-tooled wood discovered, suggests that some part of the ark still may remain on Mt. Ararat. While no final solution can be given to the ancient mystery of the survival of the ark, we must keep an open mind and have a wait-and-see attitude. The greatest discovery of modern times may be just ahead of us.

For Further Reading
THE BIBLE

Boice, J. M., *Foundations of the Christian Faith* (IVP, 1986).

Bruce, F. F., *The New Testament Documents* (IVP, 1960) *Paul, Apostle of the Free Spirit* (Paternoster, 1981).

Edwards, B. H., *Nothing But the Truth* (Evangelical Press, 1978).

Lewis, C. S., *Miracles* (Fontana, 1960).

McDowell, J., *Evidence that Demands a Verdict* (Here's Life Publications, 1979).

Machen, J. G., *The Origin of Paul's Religion* (Eerdmans, 1925).

Mickelson, A. B., *Interpreting the Bible: A Book of Basic Principles for Understanding the Scriptures* (Eerdmans, 1963).

Warfield, B. B., *The Inspiration and Authority of the Bible* (Presbyterian and Reformed).

Young, E. J., *Thy Word is Truth* (Banner of Truth, 1973).

EVOLUTION ■

Introduction

Many questions have surfaced over the years
concerning the validity of evolution and its
obvious conflict with creationism.

In this section we will bring to light many of
our reservations regarding evolution. We will
also present our reasons for questioning it as
the most accurate model or theory for
explaining the origin of life in the light of
scientific facts.

The examination of the theory of evolution
and uniformitarianism (the belief that there
were no world-wide catastrophes) begins with
several pieces of evidence which indicate either
the dating processes have serious problems or
the universe is very young. Currently accepted
opinion maintains that the earth is of the order
of 4.5 billion years old. The importance of the
earth's age is obvious, since if the earth is
young, as some creationists believe, there has
not been enough time for evolution to have
occurred.

The next few questions examine the origin of
life and some of the problems associated with it.
That whole issue is extremely speculative. No
one was there to observe the early atmospheric
conditions or to watch it happen. Without the
conditions and events described in most origin

narratives life couldn't have evolved. Yet there is, in fact, no way to prove that those conditions did occur.

After this, questions dealing with natural selection, which is the mechanism of evolution, are examined. If evolution is insufficient to account for *all* forms of life, then it simply can't be true.

The fossil record is examined next and, though often cited as the best evidence for evolution, it actually presents many problems to that position. There are no transitional forms between major stages in the evolution of life, and determining which creature is ancestral to which becomes difficult. The fossil record regarding man is in reality no more clear.

The final questions deal with several pieces of evidence which indicate the earth at one time experienced a world-wide flood. The evidence of this flood is seen in the fossil record. The flood is usually disdained by modern geology, but evidence is often overlooked which proves that geologic events occurred much more rapidly than is currently believed.

We are laymen when it comes to knowledge of scientific issues. But even when a layman researches the claims of evolutionists in light of scientific models, many questions are left unanswered.

This is not meant to be a technical treatment of the questions and issues involved, but is intended to deal with them briefly on a lay level.

Readers should be aware, as are the authors, that a book could be written on each question. This work demands that the *questions* be handled with brevity. That, by necessity, leaves many things unsaid.

It is our desire that this section will become a basis and impetus for further research by the reader.

Is the solar system really 4.5 billion years old?

Most geology or astronomy books today give 4.5 billion years as the approximate age of the solar system. This alleged age permeates modern scientific literature, although very recent evidence contradicts it. The sun, for example, if current findings are correct, couldn't have lasted 4.5 billion years.

The first scientific theory regarding the energy source for the sun had stated that meteors were falling into it to provide its fuel. This explanation was suggested shortly after Isaac Newton published his views on physics. The problem with this view of the sun's energy was that it would cause a change in the length of the year which was not observed. So much for that theory.

In about 1850, Herman von Helmholtz proposed that the energy for the sun's luminescence was caused by its very slow gravitational contraction. In other words, the sun was shrinking under its own weight. George Abell calculated:

Since the present luminosity of the sun is 4×10^{33} ergs/second, or about 10^{41} ergs/year, its contraction can have kept it shining at its present rate for a period of the order of 100 million years.[1]

Lord Kelvin also calculated the age of the sun based upon the contraction hypothesis. But unfortunately for von Helmholtz and Kelvin, this theory was published at the wrong time. Due to concepts that were then being developed in biology and geology, many scientists did not want to accept the idea of a young earth. Don L. Eicher reports:

During the period of great interest in the duration of geologic time that followed the appearance of Darwin's *Origin of Species,* Kelvin's estimates on the age of the Sun and the rate of heat loss from the Earth were by far the most influential. They were also among the very lowest. Because they were based on precise physical measurements that demanded few assumptions, they seemed irrefutable, and were acceptedly widely, if reluctantly, by most geologists. However, Darwin and his growing following of paleontologists and evolutionary biologists could not readily accept the paltry time span that Kelvin allowed because their theories required time of a far greater order of magnitude. Their opponents were well aware of this also. Kelvin's drastic curtailment of geologic time amounted to a flat renunciation of organic evolution through natural selection.[2]

Eicher continues:

Darwin could only admit that Kelvin's data constituted a formidable objection to natural selection. In the confused intellectual climate in which Darwin penned later editions of the *Origin,* he retreated from his original firm position on natural selection. He removed concrete references to enormous time spans and he attempted to compromise his previously extremely slow evolution rates. In short, his whole theoretical structure had become shaky owing to attempted adjustments to the arguments of Jenkins and Kelvin.[3]

With the discovery of radioactivity in 1896, geologists quickly began to "date" the earth.

Radioactivity was indicating that the earth was billions of years old. Well, if the earth was that old, then so must be the sun. That presented scientists with a problem: They needed some type of energy source which would allow the sun to shine constantly for around 4.5 billion years. They proposed that hydrogen fusion, the same process which occurs in hydrogen bombs, was responsible for the sun's energy. Since that time, science students have been taught that the sun is simply a large hydrogen bomb.

When two hydrogen atoms fuse or join together to form helium, a little subatomic particle called a neutrino is given off. Neutrinos are difficult to detect but they can be recorded if the detectors are placed in the bottom of mines. The number of neutrinos detected is only about four per month or about one-tenth of the number expected if, in the solar interior, hydrogen fusion were occurring.[4] What this means is that the energy of the sun is *not* coming from nuclear fusion. What then is it coming from?

In 1979, J. A. Eddy and A. A. Boornazian reported that the sun had been shrinking for at least the last 400 years.[5] Dunham and others performed similar measurements and also concluded that the sun is shrinking.[6] If this is true, then the sun just may not be as old as is taught since it would appear that Helmholtz and Kelvin's conclusion about the young age of the solar system is being supported by the most recent evidence.

∎ NOTES

[1]George Abell, *Exploration of the Universe*, Chicago: Holt Rinehart and Winston, 1969, p. 561.

[2]Don L. Eicher, *Geologic Time,* Englewood Cliffs: Prentice-Hall, 1976, p. 15.

[3]Ibid., p. 16.

[4]Hilton Hinderliter, *The Shrinking Sun: A Creationist's Prediction, Its Verification and the Resulting Implications for Theories of Origins.*

[5]J. A. Eddy and A. A. Boornazian, "Secular Decrease in the Solar Diameter, 1836-1953," *Bulletin of the American Astronomical Society,* 1979, p. 437.

[6]David W. Dunham, et al., "Observations of a Probable Change in the Solar Radius Between 1715 and 1979," *Science,* V 210 (December 12, 1980), p. 1243.

Does uranium dating work?

Uranium dating, as we are defining it, actually includes four different dating techniques, two of which don't really use uranium. Two types of uranium, called isotopes, are uranium 235 and uranium 238. Uranium 235 decays into lead 207, while uranium 238 decays into lead 206. In thorium dating, an isotope of thorium, thorium 232, decays into lead 208. The lead-lead method of dating is based upon the ratio of lead 207 to lead 206.

Significant assumptions affect each of these dating methods. First, to date an event, one must know how rapidly the original isotope decays into the final isotope. For instance, if one doesn't know how rapidly uranium 238 changes into lead 206, there is no way to tell how old the rock is. This rate of decay, known as the half-life, can be measured in a laboratory.

Second, you must be able to measure how much uranium of a given type a rock contains and how much of the daughter product (lead

206, in the case of uranium 238) the rock has. This information also can be measured in a lab.

Third, you must know the original ratio of parent to daughter isotopes. This is hard to verify.

For instance, it takes 4.5 billion years for half of the uranium 238 to change into lead 206. If you find a rock that has 50% uranium 238 and 50 percent lead 206, you could tell how old it is only if you assumed that all of the lead was originally uranium. It would then be calculated to be 4.5 billion years old. However, if I had manufactured that rock last week, by mixing equal portions of lead 206 and uranium 238, the rock would be one week old, not 4.5 billion years old. By the same token, if you can't be sure what the original constitution of the rock was, there would be no way to know its age. If a rock truly is 300 million years old, how can we be positive as to the original make-up of the rock? There was no one around to take measurements for us.

The fourth assumption in these dating methods is that the rock has not been altered in such a manner as to remove the lead or uranium. This also is hard to verify. If chemical reactions occurred which removed uranium or added lead, then the rock would date older. If the opposite occurred, the rock would date younger.

Kalervo Rankama, talking about whether these assumptions have been confirmed in tests that have been made, stated:

No radioactive minerals have been analyzed that satisfy all the requirements. Consequently, errors are liable to creep into the calculated lead ages.[1]

Returning to our four dating methods, the examples given on the following table will illustrate effectively the "errors" Rankama is speaking of.

The first entry in the table essentially says that the rock is both two billion years old and one billion years old at the same time. You can't be ten years old and twenty years old at the same time, so it is unlikely that a rock can be, either. The last entry shows a spread of two billion years for the age of the rock!

A creationist would argue that the lack of consistency shown in the table and in the previously cited dates indicates serious problems with the dating processes. Evolutionists disagree saying these discrepancies are indicative only of poorly met initial conditions or of alteration of the rocks since their deposition. *Time* magazine chides the creationist position by stating:

Other radioactive methods have been used to date earlier epochs, like the age of the earth and in a variety of trials they have produced a consistent pattern. The creationist argument is a bit like claiming that because some trains are cancelled and others run way off schedule, the basic timetable is totally inaccurate.[6]

Is this, in reality, all the creationist is doing? Does the consistency, if there is consistency, prove that radioactive dates are valid? The answer must be no. Chemical processes occurring in nature are capable of systematic removal of either lead or uranium. These processes will profoundly alter the date of a given rock. Rocks often are found which yield extremely old ages even though we know that the true age is young since it was observed being deposited. If this is so, how can we be

AGE IN MILLIONS OF YEARS

Material	Location	Dating Technique			Reference	
		U^{235}	U^{238}	Th^{223}	Lead-Lead	
Monazite		1360	1640	1180	2010	2
Granite	South Africa	330	356	238	530	3
Granite	Ontario	1030	1050	390	1090	3
Granite	Colorado	624	707	313	980	3
Granite	Arizona	630	770	271	1210	3
Granite	Colorado	925	1130	530	1540	3
Monazite		2170	2380	2100	2570	4
Monazite		1590	1420	995	1170	4
Monazite		950	930	690	880	4
Monazite		930	915	900	880	4
Monazite		390	410	440	540	4
Zircon	Ontario	1030	1050	390	1090	5
Beolite	Colorado	3180	2065	1100	1640	5

sure of the date given to a rock whose true age is unknown?

Another possibility which would allow internal inconsistency with radioactive dates is the idea that the rates of radioactive decay might have changed in the past. Naturalistic scientists will criticize this suggestion by saying that there is no evidence of such an occurrence. However, many of them are guilty of the same type of reasoning. Haldane, an evolutionist, was forced to suggest that the laws of physics and chemistry were different in the past when life originated from what they are now.[7] Dirac, a world renowned physicist, suggested that the force of gravity was greater in the past.[8] Currently, many evolutionists ascribe properties to matter which cannot be verified or refuted but have not been observed in the laboratory. (See Mechanistic or materialistic universe?) Thus it is possible for the radioactive dates to be perfectly consistent and yet perfectly wrong.

■ NOTES

[1]Kalervo Rankama, *Isotope Geology,* New York: McGraw-Hill Book Co., 1956, p. 379.

[2]A. J. Burger, L.O. Nicolaysen, and L. H. Ahrens, "Controlled Leaching of Monazites," *Journal of Geophysical Research,* Vol. 72, No. 14, p. 3587.

[3]G. R. Tilton et al., "Isotopic Ages of Zircon from Granites and Pegmatites," Transactions, *American Geophysical Union,* Vol. 38 (1957), p. 364.

[4]Burger, Nicolaysen and Ahrens, op. cit., p. 3588.

[5]George R. Tilton, "The Interpretation of Lead Age Discrepancies by Acid Washing Experiments," Transactions, *American Geophysical Union,* Vol. 37(1957), p. 226.

[6]Kenneth M. Pierce, "Putting Darwin Back in the Dock," *Time,* March 16, 1981, p. 81.

[7]See A. E. Wilder Smith, *Man's Origin, Man's Destiny,* Wheaton, Harold Shaw, 1968, p. 168.

[8]P. A. M. Dirac, "The Cosmological Constants," *Nature,* February 20, 1937.

Does potassium-argon dating work?

The potassium-argon method of dating makes the same assumptions as all other dating methods. It is based upon the decay of a certain type or isotope of potassium to argon. In order to date an object with this method, one must know how much argon and potassium are in the rock today, how much was in the rock when it was formed, and how rapidly the potassium changes to argon. One must further assume that no argon has escaped from or entered the rock since its formation.

Once again the difficulty lies in the determination of the initial content of the rock. Since there was no one around to measure the potassium and argon when the rock was formed, the third assumption must be satisfied by making an educated guess. Since argon is an inert gas, meaning it won't form chemical bonds with other elements, most users of the potassium-argon method assume that when a lava flow occurs, all argon escapes from the rock. Thus one needs, so the theory goes, only to measure the amount of potassium and argon presently in the rock to find out how long it took for that amount of argon to collect.

However as Kalervo Rankama says,

While the potassium-argon method became definitely established as a geological tool, it still suffered from the fact that the ages were not always correct.[1]

Some examples of the failure of the potassium-argon dating method will show the absurdities one runs into when believing in radioactive dating processes.

C. S. Noble and J. J. Naughton used potassium-argon to date an underwater lava flow. Judging by the unweathered appearance of the flow, they judged that it was less than 200 years old. However, when they dated the rock using potassium-argon, the rock dated from 12 to 21 million years old.[2] Obviously, the method didn't work.

Lovering and Richards extracted different minerals from the same volcanic structure and dated them. For the Kimberlite pipe in South Africa, two different minerals yielded ages of 68 million years and 142 million years. That's a large variation when they should have yielded approximately the same age. They then did the same experiment on the Breccia pipe from Australia and obtained ages ranging from 121 million years to 911 million years.[3] Take your pick.

The 1800-1801 Kaupulehu lava flow in Hawaii, a flow which man watched coming out of the ground, yielded potassium-argon ages of 1 to 2.4 billion years. This lava flow is less than 200 years old! The same flow, when dated by helium dating, yielded ages of 140 million years to 670 million years.[4]

The Salt Lake Crater on Oahu yielded potassium-argon dates of 92-147 million years, 140-680 million years, 930-1580 million years, 1230-1960 million years, 1290-2050 million years, and 1360-1900 million years. How old do you want it to be?[5]

Here's one final example of potassium-argon dating. In the Auckland volcanic field of New Zealand, the lava flows have buried the forests at the base of the volcanoes. As in Pompeii, the trees, being encased in lava, were not destroyed, but were preserved. This presents a tremendous opportunity to test two dating methods against each other. By dating the wood with carbon14 and the lava with potassium-argon one can compare the results. McDougall, Polach and Stipp note:

Whole rock samples from sixteen volcanoes were measured by the (potassium-argon) method, and direct or indirect radiocarbon dating control was available for eleven of them. With few exceptions, anomalously old, but often internally consistent (potassium-argon) dates were found for the lavas. Additional radiocarbon dating was then carried out on several wood samples; with one notable exception, the new results were consistent with the earlier determinations. For the volcanic island of Rangitoto, the radiocarbon, geological and botanical evidence unequivocally shows that it was active and was probably built during the last 1000 years. The (potassium-argon) dates on basalts from this volcano range from 145,000 to 465,000 years.[6]

Obviously, there are flaws in potassium-argon dating.

■ NOTES

[1] Kalervo Rankama, *Progress in Isotope Geology,* New York, Interscience Publishers, 1963, p. 43.

[2] C. S. Noble and J. J. Naughton, "Deep-Ocean Basalts: Inert Gas Content and Uncertainties in Age Dating," *Science,* Vol. 162, pp. 265-266.

[3] J. F. Lovering and J. R. Richards, "Potassium Argon Age Study of Possible Lower-Crust and Upper-Mantle Inclusions in Deep-Seated Intrusions," *Journal of Physical Research,* Vol. 69, p. 4897.

[4] J. G. Funkenhouser and John J. Naughton, "Radiogenic Helium and Argon in Ultramatic Inclusions from Hawaii," *Journal of Geophysical Research,* Vol. 73 #14, p. 4602.

[5] Ibid.

[6] Ianougall, H. A. Polach and J. J. Stipp, "Excess Radiogenic Argon in Young Subaerial Basalts from the Auckland Volcanic Field, New Zealand," *Geochimica et Cosmochimica Acta,* Vol. 33, p. 1485.

Does carbon 14 work?

The carbon 14 dating technique is certainly the most well-known dating method. It, too, has certain assumptions which must be *fulfilled* or the method won't yield accurate results.

Carbon 14 is produced in the upper atmosphere when an atom of nitrogen 14 is struck by a cosmic ray. This changes the nitrogen to carbon 14. The carbon 14 then disperses throughout the atmosphere and is absorbed by the plants by photosynthesis. When an animal eats a plant, part of the carbon 14 is then incorporated into its body. A carnivorous animal eating that animal also gets carbon 14 into its body. This process continues, so the theory goes, until every living creature is radioactive to exactly the same degree.

When a plant or animal dies it quits assimilating carbon 14 into its body. As time passes, the carbon 14 decays back to nitrogen 14. This means that the older the organic material is the less carbon 14 it will have. Thus one can date the object if certain conditions are met.

First, as with all dating methods, one must know how much carbon 14 the animal or plant had when it died. If an animal was somehow able to avoid getting any carbon 14 into its system, it would date very old if you assumed that it died with the usual amount of carbon 14 in its body.

Usually the assumption is made that the level of atmospheric carbon 14 has been constant over the last 20 to 30,000 years.[1] But in order for this assumption to be true, the level of atmospheric nitrogen and the rate of cosmic ray bombardment also must have been constant over the last 30,000 years. This last assumption seems rather uncertain since the first measurements of the cosmic ray flux were made in the early part of the twentieth century. It seems rather bold to extrapolate the results of approximately eighty years of measurements to cover the last 30,000 years. Even so, this is the assumption that is made.

The second assumption of carbon dating is that we can measure the proportion of normal carbon 12 to the carbon 14. This assumption is no problem since these measurements can be carried out with a tremendous amount of precision.

The final assumption is that the rate of radioactive decay of carbon 14 does not change. If carbon 14 decayed either faster or slower in the past, then the age obtained by using today's decay rate would be wrong.

The interesting thing about the rate of carbon 14 decay is that it can be changed in the laboratory. John Lynde Anderson set up an experiment in which he altered the electric charge on a plate containing carbon 14. He reports,

The mean during the 90 V+ conditions is therefore more than nine standard deviations lower than was observed at 90 V−.[2]

What this means is that the rate of decay was radically altered by applying different electrical potentials to the carbon 14. The implications of this are far-reaching. For example, every time an electrical storm passed over an object in the ground, it could alter the rate of decay of the carbon 14. The electrical charge in the clouds and on the earth at such times would produce the same effect as Anderson produced in the laboratory.

So much for the theoretical considerations. There is no better way to illustrate the problems in carbon 14 than to show some examples.

Yale University dated an antler three different times and got three different ages—5,340 years, 9,310 years, and 10,320 years.[3] The University of Michigan dated two specimens from the same stratigraphic positions (which means they should date the same) as being 1,430 and 2,040 years old.[4] A piece of bark dated by both the University of Chicago and the University of

Michigan yielded ages of 1,168 years and 2,200 years.[5] Carbon 14, when applied to a mastodon, indicated it died from the outside-in over a 750-year period. The outside of the tusk dated at 7,820 years since death, while the interior of the tusk died 750 years later.[6] Imagine the agony of that poor animal!

Charles Reed notes,

What bids to become a classic example of C[14] irresponsibility is the 6,000-year spread of eleven determinations for Jarmo, a prehistoric village in northern Iraq, which, on the basis of all archaeological evidence, was not occupied for more than 500 consecutive years.[7]

Examples such as these are not difficult to find. And after seeing them, one must wonder how well carbon 14 dating works.

■ NOTES

[1]Kalervo Rankama, *Isotope Geology,* New York: McGraw-Hill Book Co., 1956, p. 226.

[2]John Lynde Anderson, "Non-Poisson Distributions Observed During Counting of Certain Carbon-14 Labeled Organic (Sub) Monolayers," *Journal of Physical Chemistry,* Vol. 76, No. 24 (1972), p. 3610.

[3]G. W. Barendsen, E. S. Deevey, and L. J. Gralenski, "Yale Natural Radiocarbon Measurements," *Science,* Vol. 126, p. 911. See sample No. Y-159, Y-159-1 and Y-159-2.

[4]H. R. Crane and James B. Griffin, "University of Michigan Radiocarbon Dates III," *Science,* Vol. 128, p. 1120. See samples No. M-663, and M-664.

[5]H. R. Crane, "University of Michigan Radiocarbon Dates II," *Science,* Vol. 124, p. 666. See sample M-19.

[6]H. R. Crane, "University of Michigan Radiocarbon Dates II," *Science,* Vol. 127, p. 1100. See samples M-280 and M-281.

[7]Charles Reed, "Animal Domestication in the Prehistoric Near East," *Science,* Vol. 130, p. 1630.

Is there evidence of instantaneous creation?

Over the last ten to fifteen years, evidence has been gathered which seems to indicate that the earth was created in an instant. The evidence comes from the study of a feature of many igneous rocks. The radiohalo, found throughout various minerals, is a discoloration of the rock, caused by the radioactive decay of a small speck of a radioactive element contained in the rock.

When a small speck or inclusion of a substance, such as uranium 238, is trapped in the rock, the uranium emits alpha particles which destroy the crystal structure of the radio-active mineral. Since the alpha particles are emitted from the uranium with a particular speed, the alpha particles can travel only a certain distance through the rock before they stop. When the alpha particles stop, they discolor the rock.

Since the alpha particles are emitted in all directions, a spherical shell of discoloration is produced.

While uranium is decaying to lead, it passes through fifteen steps. When an atom of uranium emits an alpha particle, the atom no longer is uranium but becomes thorium which in turn gives off a particle and turns into another element.

During this process alpha particles with five distinct velocities are given off. Because of this, when uranium is trapped in a rock a set of five concentric discolorations of the rock will occur. The size of each halo is determined by the speed of the alpha particle, for each element in the decay chain has emitted particles with a specified velocity. Thus if one finds a halo of a certain radius, he often can determine what element formed the halo from the radius alone.

Polonium 218, polonium 214 and polonium 210 are the radioactive substances which are responsible for three halos in the characteristic five-ringed uranium halo. These three isotopes of polonium are found today only mixed up with uranium 238. This is because polonium decays so rapidly that it cannot be stored for more than a few minutes. The only reason it even exists is that it is constantly being formed by the decay of uranium.

Two factors are required before a halo can form.

1. A small speck of a radioactive substance must be included in the molten rock before it cools.
2. The rock must solidify and form a crystal before all of the radioactivity is ended.

Because of these considerations, it was surprising when two- and three-ring halos were discovered in a size which indicated they had been formed by the three isotopes of polonium. Since polonium 218 has a half-life of only three minutes, most polonium is almost entirely gone within thirty minutes. Therefore, to find a polonium 218 halo without any evidence of a uranium halo seemed to indicate that the molten rock solidified within thirty minutes of the formation of the polonium 218, and since the only known source of polonium 218 is from the decay of uranium, the only apparent source of that polonium would be by creation.

The situation gets more interesting with

polonium 214 halos—the two-ringed halos
mentioned above. The half-life of polonium 214
is 0.000164 second. This means that the rock
would have had to cool in less than
one-thousandth of a second after the polonium
214 was created. No known process of nature
can cool and solidify a rock that rapidly.

Is it possible that this proves God created the
earth in an instant?

Is coal young in age?

Radiohalos, the circular discolorations in rocks
produced by the decay of a speck of a
radioactive element, severely challenged
currently accepted ideas of geologic time. We
already have seen that polonium halos indicate
that an instantaneous creation of the earth is
the most reasonable conclusion. Some double
halos found by R. V. Gentry and others
indicate that coal, believed to be approximately
100 million years old, is in reality only a few
thousand years old.

When a radiohalo forms, it always is very
nearly circular in shape. This is because the
alpha particles emitted by the radioactive speck
are able to travel the same distance through the
rock in any direction. When the particle stops,
it destroys the chemical structure of the region,
causing the discoloration.

Gentry, et al,[1] discovered a double halo—an
oval halo covered by a circular one—in coalified
wood fragments, from coal believed to be 100
million years old. Since halos are circular

discolorations, the oval halo was believed to have been originally formed as a circle and when the tree was compressed into coal, the circular halo also was compressed into the oval shape. Afterward, a new circular halo began forming on top of the older oval one.

If this interpretation of the double halos is correct, then the uranium, which caused the halo, had to have been in the wood prior to the time the wood turned into coal. So, Gentry reasoned, if we date the uranium in the tiny speck which caused the halo, we could determine the age of the coal. His team did this and concluded:

Such extraordinary values (the dates) admit the possibility that both the initial (uranium) infiltration and coalification would possibly have occurred within the past several thousand years.[2]

In other words, the coal had to have been formed only a few thousand years ago. Because of the importance of this conclusion, Gentry's team conducted the same survey on coalified wood found in the Devonian Chatanooga shale. This shale commonly is believed to be around 350 million years old, yet Gentry's study showed that the coal in the shale couldn't possibly be that old.[3]

Thus if one wishes to believe in radioactive dating, he also must accept these dates which show young ages for the coal and shale. If one wishes to reject these dates, he also should reject all the other dates. One should not simply accept the dates he wants to and reject those that disagree with his personal belief.

If you believe that dating is valid, how do you

explain the young ages given by Gentry's group?

■ NOTES

[1] R. V. Gentry, et al., "Radiohalos in Coalified Wood: New Evidence Relating to the Time of Uranium Introduction and Coalification," *Science*, Vol. 194, p. 315-318.
[2] Ibid., p. 317.
[3] Ibid.

How long can the mountains last?

Erosion, a fascinating process, occurs by a variety of means and gradually is wearing the land down. Rainfall, as it soaks through the soil to the rocks below, picks chemicals out of the soil which break the rocks into various chemical compounds. These compounds then become soil. However, as this new soil is being formed below the present soil, the present soil is being carried away by the rain waters as they flow down a hill into the creeks and streams. From there the soil is carried downstream to the ocean where it is deposited on the bottom of the ocean.

This, in a simplified form, is erosion. Over a long period of time, the mountains and plains, the entire continent, would be worn down to the level of the sea.

How fast does this process occur? An even better question: How does one even estimate the speed of erosion?

There are several methods of estimating erosion rates over a continent. However, the best method probably is to measure the amount of sediment in the water at the mouths of rivers around the continent, then estimating how much water flows out of the rivers each year. By establishing these two figures, one then can estimate how much dirt and sand are carried to the sea each year. This would allow one to determine the average rate of erosion.

Several authorities have estimated erosion rates based upon the technique described above. Generally, the estimates vary somewhat for they depend upon the assumptions of the investigator. Sheldon Judson estimated that the rates of erosion were as low as 2.4 centimeters per 1000 years,[1] while Karl Turekian estimated that the continents are being lowered at the rate of 6 centimeters per 1000 years.[2] These rates are so slow that you will not see the change in the shape of the earth in your lifetime.

This creates a problem, however, if the earth really is as old as currently is believed. Judson remarks:

Whether we use the rate of erosion prevailing before or after man's advent, our figures pose the problem of why our continents have survived. If we accept the rate of sediment production as 10^{10} metric tons per year (the pre-human intervention figure) then the continents are being lowered at the rate of 2.4 cm per 1,000 years. At this rate the ocean basins, with a volume of $1.37 \times 10^8 m^3$, would be filled in 340 million years. The geologic record indicates that this has never happened in the past, and there is no reason to believe it will happen in the geologically forseeable future. Furthermore, at present rates of erosion, the continents, which now average 875 m in elevation, would be reduced to close to sea level in about 34 million years. So we reason that the continents have always been high enough to supply sediments to the oceans.[3]

Judson's 340 million years are less than one tenth of the estimated age of the earth. Yet his calculations, based upon present-day measurements, indicate that the ocean basins could have been filled more than ten times at the current rate of sedimentation. His data further show that the continents would not exist after 34 million years. Unfortunately, in spite of experimental evidence to the contrary, Judson concludes that the continents always have been high enough to provide sediments to the oceans.

Turekian notes:

The corresponding rate of lowering of the continents by erosion, if no further mountain building elevates part of them again (as must of course be the case), is 6 centimeters per 1,000 years. Since the average elevation of the continents is 800 meters, it would take about 13 million years to lower the continents to sea level. We have geological evidence for lands and mountains for billions of years, so we conclude that the continents are renewed by mountain building and continental uplift fast enough to keep up with the erosion rate.[4]

Dott and Batten remark that,

Some mode of crustal rejuvenation is inescapable. Otherwise, continents long ago would have been eroded permanently to sea level; present rates of denudation could do the job in a mere 10 or 20 million years.[5]

One must notice in the statements of these authorities from where the continental uplift comes. None presents experimental evidence to justify his belief in rapid uplift. Each conclusion is based upon a confidence that the earth is vastly older than the erosion rates would allow. This confidence, in turn, is based upon a confidence in the dating methods which, as we have shown, are anything but conclusive.

It is an inescapable deduction that if the dating processes aren't telling us the true age of the earth, the erosion rates certainly would limit the age of the earth.

■ NOTES

[1] Sheldon Judson, "Erosion of the Land or What's Happening to Our Continents," *American Scientist*, Vol. 56, 4. p. 371, 372.

[2] Karl K. Turekian, *Oceans*, Englewood Cliffs: Prentice-Hall, 1976, p. 50.

[3] Sheldon Judson, lec. cit. p. 371, 372.

[4] Karl K. Turekian, *Oceans*, p. 50.

[5] Robert H. Dott and Roger L. Batten, *Evolution of the Earth*, St. Louis, McGraw-Hill Book Co., 1971, p. 476.

Are there problems with the galactic clusters?

A study of galactic clusters raises another problem with the old universe theory. Just as stars are gathered into a large cluster (which astronomers call a galaxy), galaxies too are gathered into groups called clusters. Studies of these galactic clusters reveal an apparent lack of enough gravitational force to hold them together for very long.[1]

An astronomer can estimate the mass of a galaxy because the mass is related to the galaxy's brightness. Once the masses of all the galaxies for a cluster have been calculated, the gravitational force holding the cluster together also can be calculated.

The next step in the study of the cluster is to calculate the relative velocities of the galaxies in relation to each other. This can be accomplished because the light emitted by the stars of a galaxy can tell us how fast the galaxy is moving. Once these two items—the estimated gravitational force and the velocities—are derived, they can be compared to see if there is enough gravity to hold the cluster together.

The surprising result: There doesn't appear to be enough mass in the clusters to overcome the velocities with which the galaxies are moving. If the measured mass of the galaxies is anywhere near correct, the galactic clusters should have dispersed long ago and should not still exist.

One example of this "missing mass" is seen in a study of the Coma Cluster. For this cluster to be stable enough to exist for its alleged 10 billion years, it would have to have seven times more mass than is measured.[2] The huge Virgo cluster, which can be seen in the constellation Virgo, contains at least 1,000 galaxies. Yet it lacks 98 percent of the mass needed to hold the cluster together.[3] In other words, if these clusters are indeed billions of years old, why are they still in existence?

∎ NOTES

[1] For a discussion of this topic, see *Age of the Cosmos*, by Harold S. Slusher, San Diego Institute for Creation Research, 1980, p. 7-14. See also "The Extra-galactic Ferment," Anonymous, Mosaic 9:18-27, May/June 1978, cited in William R. Corliss, *The Mysterious Universe*, Glen Arm: The Source Book Project, 1980, p. 586.
[2] Harold S. Slusher, *Age of the Cosmos*, p. 12.
[3] Ibid., p. 12.

Are the spiral galaxies young in age?

Much of the support for an old universe comes from the measured movement of the galaxies. Everywhere in the universe, galaxies are speeding away from us. Apparently they travel faster, the farther away they are. Calculations have shown that all the galaxies would have been together at one point in space, 10 to 15 billion years ago, if they ever were together. It was at this time (10 to 15 billion years ago), scientists say that the big bang occurred, sending all matters away from a central place. This is the usual explanation for the galaxies.

There is, however, one flaw in this picture of the universe: The galaxies themselves appear young. Almost everyone has seen photos of some of the beautiful spiral galaxies. It is the spiral structure itself which shows that the galaxies must be young—at least far younger than the estimated 10-billion-year age of the universe.

As the stars orbit around the galactic center, the stars closer to the center revolve faster than the more-distant stars. For instance, a star 8,000 light years from the galactic center will revolve approximately 2.8 orbits for every one orbit completed by a star 16,000 light years from the center. By the same token, a star 16,000 light years from the center will complete 2.8 revolutions for every one revolution of a star 32,000 light years from the center.

Therefore, by the time the most distant star in the spiral has completed one revolution, the inner star has nearly completed eight.

The effect of these different rotation rates is

that the spiral arms soon will wrap themselves around the galactic center until the spiral arms no longer are noticeable.

If the Milky Way, our galaxy, is 4.5 billion years old, the same as the accepted age of the earth, then the sun would have completed twenty-two revolutions, at 200 million years per revolution, around the galaxy. A star in our spiral arm half the distance from the galactic center as we are would have completed nearly sixty-two revolutions around the galaxy. The spirals in our own galaxy, therefore, should not be visible. Yet they are. The same is true for other distant galaxies. By this time in the universe's history (assuming old universe estimates are correct), the spirals should no longer exist. The fact that they do indicates that the age of the universe is far younger.

Is there controversy in the history of the origin of life?

In the Middle Ages, how life originated was not considered a problem. Everyone knew that in the beginning, God created all life. They also "knew" that life spontaneously arose from non-living things. Maggots arose from decaying meat, frogs from stagnant ponds, earthworms from manure, mice from warm moist soil and insects from the morning dew.

The belief in spontaneous generation of life predominated from the time of Aristotle until the middle of the nineteenth century. The first challenge to this belief came in 1668 when

Francesco Redi, an Italian physician, carried out a simple experiment which indicated that maggots were not the spontaneous product of decaying meat. Redi placed a piece of meat in a jar covered with stretched Neapolitan muslin. Although the meat decayed, no maggots arose in it. Thus Redi ascribed the "spontaneous generation" of maggots to poor observation. His conclusion: Meat merely provided a nest for the development of the insects.

In spite of this evidence, Redi refused to give up the idea of spontaneous generation entirely. He continued to believe in the spontaneous generation of intestinal and wood worms.

About this same time, Anton Van Leeuwenhoek, a Dutch scientist, discovered the world of bacteria and inspired many other scientists to construct microscopes and search for bacteria. These tiny plants and animals were found everywhere. In fact, the presence of bacteria appeared to support those who believed in spontaneous generation. It was easy to watch spontaneous generation occur because, when a decomposable substance was put in a warm place, the bacteria soon appeared where there had been none.

Leeuwenhoek and his followers did not agree with this view, so Louis Joblot, one of Leeuwenhoek's followers, boiled a hay broth for fifteen minutes and placed the broth into two separate containers. One was left open to the air while the other was sealed before it cooled. This experiment was an attempt to test the idea that the bacteria got into the broth from the air. The sealed jar developed no bacteria while the open jar teemed with them. However, Joblot's experimental evidence failed to convince the world.

An interesting argument developed in the late eighteenth century between John T. Needham, a Scottish preacher, and Abbe Spallanzani, an Italian scientist. Both were performing experiments similar to Joblot's, but they were reaching opposite conclusions concerning the viability of spontaneous generation.

Needham was a vitalist. Vitalists believed that matter contained a vital force or principle which caused spontaneous generation. Needham performed experiments in which he boiled broths and sealed them. After a few days, micro-organisms would be present. These experiments, he claimed, proved the possibility of spontaneous generation.

Spallanzani, believing that air carried the germs of micro-organisms, conducted experiments in which the boiled broth didn't produce bacteria. Furthermore, he charged Needham with improperly sterilizing equipment. That was why Needham's experiments failed, he said.

Needham, on the other hand, responded that Spallanzani had over-heated his broths, thus destroying the vital force in the broth. He denied that he had under-heated his broths.

J. H. Rush, concerning the argument between these two, remarks,

The trend of the argument is curious. It illustrates beautifully the tendency to believe what we want to believe.[1]

The reason the argument couldn't be settled was that the results obtained were inconsistent. In 1859, the year Darwin published *The Origin of Species,* F. Pouchet published a work of nearly 700 pages in which he defended the vital principle and spontaneous generation. All his experimental work supported his view. Because of this, the French Academy of Sciences offered a prize to the first person who could devise an experiment which would settle the question.

Three years later, in 1862, Louis Pasteur published the proof everyone had been waiting for. In a brilliant series of experiments, Pasteur showed that micro-organisms do live in the air, an idea Pouchet had ridiculed, and proved that as long as micro-organisms in the air were kept out of the broths, no molds appeared.

George Wald, speaking of the downfall of spontaneous generation, says,

We tell this story to beginning students of biology as though it represents a triumph of reason over mysticism. In fact it is very nearly the opposite. The reasonable view was to believe in spontaneous generation; the only alternative, to believe in a single, primary act of supernatural creation. There is no third position. For this reason, many scientists a century ago chose to regard the belief in spontaneous generation as a philosophical necessity. It is a symptom of the philosophical poverty of our time that this necessity is no longer appreciated. Most modern biologists, having reviewed, with satisfaction, the downfall of the spontaneous generation hypothesis, yet unwilling to accept the alternative belief in special creation, are left with nothing.[2]

Thus ends the story of the superstitious beliefs in spontaneous generation—or so we are told. Actually, the story has not ended. Philosophically, those who don't want to accept the idea that God created the world still are forced to explain the fact of life without Him. Therefore, the modern belief in spontaneous generation has taken a new form. A. I. Oparin, a Russian biochemist, who propounded a theory of the chemical origin of life, said,

A careful survey of the experimental evidence reveals, however, that it tells us nothing about the impossibility of generation of life at some other epoch or under some other conditions.[3]

So instead of destroying the belief in spontaneous generation, Pasteur merely forced the issue to a point where neither side can disprove the other, at least in a conclusive manner. This, too, reminds one of what Rush said:

It illustrates beautifully the tendency to believe what we want to believe.[4]

However, even though neither side can disprove the other, we will see how improbable is the origin of life by chance, as suggested by Oparin and others. We also will see that there is not enough time for a purely mechanistic origin of life. Neither is there conclusive evidence that life formed in the manner postulated, nor evidence that the conditions postulated existed.

■ NOTES

[1]J. H. Rush, *The Dawn of Life*, Garden City: Hanover House, 1957, p. 93.

[2]George Wald, "The Origin of Life," *Scientific American*, Vol. 191, #2, p. 46.

[3]A. I. Oparin, *Origin of Life,* translated by Sergius
    Morgulis, New York: Dover Publications, 1965, p. 29.
[4]Rush, op. cit.

Is there enough time?

If the mechanistic view of life is correct, then
the origin of life can be explained only by the
chance formation of amino acids, followed by
the chance union of amino acids to form
proteins. However, the chance formation of
even the smallest useful protein would be a rare
event. Because of this, large spans of time
would be needed to improve the probability
that useful proteins had been formed.

The story often is told of a group of
gibberish-typing monkeys who, by chance, will
produce Gibbon's *Decline and Fall of the
Roman Empire* if they type long enough.
Nobody ever seems to ask, "How long must
they type?"

A typical statement in this kind of literature
is:

So that if we had amino acids, we then would have proteins,
and if we had proteins we would be well along the road to
life. Given trillions upon trillions of possibilities for chemical
combinations, given a few million years for it all to happen,
the components of life would have appeared. And once that
had been accomplished, once the bricks and the stones and
the lumber for the building of life were present, then all
that would have been required were a few more million
years for life to actually appear.[1]

The current most widely accepted estimate
for the age of the universe is around 10 billion

years,[2] while the earth is believed to be only 4-5 billion years old. Is this enough time for the useful protein combinations to be formed?

In the case of insulin, Asimov estimated that there are 8×10^{27} (8 followed by 27 zeroes) different possible combinations of an insulin-like protein.[3] For the sake of argument, let us assume that each second that the *universe* has existed a different combination of an insulin-like protein is produced. After 10 billion years, we would have approximately 3×10^{17} (3 followed by 17 zeroes) different combinations, or approximately one ten-billionth of all the possible combinations of insulin. To be positive that the one combination which the body uses is produced, we would need to wait an additional 10 billion times the presently supposed age of the universe. In other words, we would need to wait one hundred quintillion years longer until all combinations of insulin had been produced.

In the case of hemoglobin, the chance formation of life is even less probable. Asimov estimates 135 followed by 165 zeroes as the different combinations of hemoglobin.[4] Once again only a limited number of combinations are useful. This time let's assume that 10^{100} (10 followed by 100 zeroes) different combinations are produced each second the universe has existed. Actually, this would be impossible because the total number of atoms in the observable universe[5] is only 10^{78}. Thus our hemoglobin factory would consume approximately 10 sextillion universes every second, just to maintain this rate of production. Even so, it would take ten trillion trillion years to produce all of the different combinations of hemoglobin.

Examples like this are easy to find. It doesn't take much imagination to realize how improbable the chance formation of the smallest known virus is. DNA is composed of four smaller chemicals which are arranged in ladder-like fashion. In the smallest known virus, the DNA has only 5,000 of these small chemicals—2,500 per side of the ladder.[6] There would be approximately 10 followed by 1,505 zeroes different combinations.

Thus it would appear that there has not been enough time in the universe to explain the chance formation of life.

■ NOTES

[1]Clifford D. Sirnak, *Trilobites, Dinosaurs and Man*, New York: St. Martins Press, 1966, p. 54.

[2]Frank Wilczek, "The Cosmic Assymetry between Matter and Antimatter," *Scientific American*, Dec. 1980, p. 83.

[3]Isaac Asimov, *The Genetic Code*, New York: The New American Library, 1962, p. 92.

[4]Ibid.

[5]P. C. W. Davis, "Dirac Completes His Theory of Large Numbers," Nature 250:460, 1974, cited in *Mysterious Universe: A Handbook of Astronomical Anamalies*, compiled by William R. Corliss, published 1979 by the Source Book Project.

[6]Lawrence Lessing, *DNA: At the Core of Life Itself*, New York: Macmillan Co., 1966, p. 15.

Are probabilities against the chance formation of large biological molecules?

One of the most difficult problems facing those who accept the naturalistic origin of life is that the odds are against the chance formation of even the most simple organic molecules. The hormone, vasopressin, is a simple protein— simple as far as proteins are concerned. Vasopressin, produced in the pituitary gland, prevents the loss of too much water in the body by regulating the action of the kidneys. Further, it increases a person's blood pressure.

Chemically, vasopressin is made up of eight amino acids. These are, in order along the molecule (see Figure 1, p. 141): glycinamide, arginine, proline, cystine, asparagine, glutamine, phenylalanine, and tyrosine. The order in which these amino acids occur is extremely critical to the proper functioning of the hormone. Even a switch in position between two amino acids along the molecule will destroy the correct function.

If we were to place just these eight amino acids in a hat and draw them all out one by one, we could expect to get them in the same order as they are in vasopressin only 1 out of every 40,320 attempts. The reason is simple. When you draw out the first amino acid, there are eight possibilities. For the second choice, there are seven amino acids in the hat so there are only seven possibilities, etc. Thus, the number of possibilities for the "vasopressin-type" of hormone is $8 \times 7 \times 6 \times 5 \times 4 \times 3 \times 2 \times 1$. This equals 40,320.

The number of possibilities increases dramatically as the protein molecule gets larger. Isaac Asimov[1] estimates that the 30-amino-acid-protein, insulin, has 8,000,000,000,000,000,000,000,000,000 (eight octillion) different arrangements. He further estimates that the number of possible combinations for a 140 amino acid protein like hemoglobin is 135 followed by 165 zeroes. This is a larger number than all the atoms estimated in the universe.

Out of all these possibilities, the body can use only one arrangement. Asimov states,

Out of 40,320 possible vasopressin combinations, the body chooses just one out of eight octillion possible combinations; for one of the insulin polypeptides, the body chooses just one.

The question is no longer where the body finds the variety it needs, but how it controls the possible variety and keeps it within bounds.[2]

■ NOTES

[1]Isaac Asimov, *The Genetic Code*, New York: The New American Library, 1962, p. 92.
[2]Ibid., p. 93.

Mechanistic or materialistic universe?

Because of the problems in relying simply on chance for the origin of life, as already outlined, many scientists have rejected this mechanistic viewpoint in favor of a materialistic viewpoint. The mechanistic outlook relies on pure chance to explain the origin of life, while the materialistic position believes that evolution is inevitable whenever the conditions are right. This is because the materialist believes there are certain laws, natural laws or properties associated with matter, which overcome the problems inherent with chance.

A. I. Oparin, talking about the problems of chance, states:

All these difficulties, however, disappear, if we discard once and for all the above mechanistic conception and take the standpoint that the simplest living organisms originated gradually by a long evolutionary process of organic substance and that they represent merely definite mileposts along the general historic road of evolution of matter.[1]

He further states:

It is absolutely unthinkable that such complex structures like organisms could have been ever generated spontaneously, directly from carbon dioxide, water, oxygen, nitrogen and mineral salts. The generation of living things must have been *inevitably* preceded by a primary development on the Earth's surface of those organic substances of which organisms are constructed[2] (our emphasis).

Oparin's view, as well as that of others, is that life will arise from non-life whenever or wherever conditions are right. It is inevitable that this would occur because there are, in this view, laws of matter which would cause life to evolve. The earliest chemicals on the road to life are governed by the laws of atoms. As more complex chemicals are formed and are united into a larger structure, different laws (applicable to the larger structure) take over. Just as an atom is the basic building block of a molecule, and a molecule is the basic unit for the cell, the cell is the basic unit for the organism.

According to the materialistic viewpoint, as opposed to the mechanistic viewpoint, these different levels of organization are subject to different laws. These different laws inevitably lead matter from the non-living to the living whenever conditions are correct.

This viewpoint can be seen in what Oparin says:

This brief survey purports to show the gradual evolution of organic substances and the manner by which ever newer properties, subject to laws of a higher order, were superimposed step-by-step upon the erstwhile simple and elementary properties of matter. At first there were the simple solutions of organic substances, whose behavior was governed by the properties of their component atoms and the arrangement of those atoms in the molecular structure. But gradually as a result of growth and increased complexity of the molecules new properties have come into being and a new colloid-chemical order was imposed upon the more simple organic chemical relations. These newer properties were determined by the spatial arrangement and mutual relationship of the molecules. Even this configuration of organic matter was still insufficient to give rise to primary living things. For this, the colloidal systems in the process of their evolution had to acquire properties of a still higher order, which would permit the attainment of the next and more advanced phase in the organization of matter. In this process biological orderliness already comes into prominence. Competitive speed of growth, struggle for existence and, finally, natural selection determined such a form of material organization which is characteristic of living things of the present time.[3]

This materialistic viewpoint always is expressed analogously, not analytically. Even H. F. Blum's somewhat mathematical treatment is still little more than math by analogy.[4] The analogy is made between atoms, molecules, cells, organisms and culture with each different level exhibiting different properties than the previous stage. But the exact form of these "laws" never is outlined. The lack of an analytic form for these laws, which are supposed to govern the evolution of matter from atoms to man, makes experimental verification or refutation impossible.

If you are told that energy is equal to the mass times the square of the speed of light ($E=mc^2$), you can go into a laboratory and either prove or refute that statement. On the other hand, if you are told that there are material laws which lead to the evolution of man (or something similar) how are you to verify it? You can't. Therefore, the materialistic position is merely a philosophical point, not a scientific one. The materialist is postulating certain properties of matter which can't be observed and therefore must be accepted or rejected by faith, not on the basis of evidence or logic.

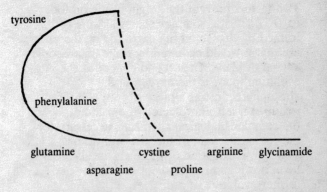

FIGURE 1: OX VASOPRESSIN

■ NOTES

[1]A. I. Oparin, *The Origin Of Life,* translated by Sergius Morgulis, New York: Dover Publications, 1965, p. 60.
[2]Ibid., p. 62.

[3]Ibid., p. 250, 251.
[4]See H. F. Blum, *Time's Arrow and Evolution*, Princeton: Princeton University Press, 1968, p. 200-219.

Is the atmosphere young in age?

The basic requirement for the chemical evolution of life is that once a certain necessary chemical is formed by chance processes, it must be preserved until all of the other necessary chemicals are formed and subsequently brought together. When this finally occurred, scientists believe, the first life appeared.

Could we observe the formation of life by chemical evolution today? Scientists say no. Two factors prevent the origin of life on today's earth. First, if a complex chemical were to be formed by chance on the earth today, the odds are that it would be eaten by some microscopic animal or plant. The second danger to chemical evolution today is the oxygen in the atmosphere. Just as a piece of iron will rust (oxidize) if left unprotected in our atmosphere, the complex biological chemicals necessary for the chemical origin of life also will oxidize if left alone. The oxidation of these chemicals breaks them down and makes them useless for the further evolution of life.

Therefore, if life originated by chance on earth, these two hindrances had to have been absent. Since no other life was present when the first life was formed, the chemicals were safe from bacteria. None was around to eat the chemicals. Oxygen however, is a different matter. As long as oxygen was in the atmosphere, no evolution could occur. This is the primary evidence cited for the early atmosphere being different from the present atmosphere. However, one must first assume evolution occurred before one can say that the early atmosphere of the earth lacked oxygen.

As we have seen, if the early atmosphere had free oxygen, no evolution could occur. But this provides no evidence for what was in the early atmosphere. J. H. Rush tells how the composition of the early atmosphere is determined. He says,

Like other questions of the earth's beginning, the formation of its atmosphere follows from and is colored by the theory chosen to account for the origin of the solar system. Any serious theory, however, involves conditions that must have led to the accumulation of an atmosphere of gas around any planetary body massive enough to hold it. Just what gases were present, and in what proportions, are questions for informed speculation rather than any real certainty.[1]

William Rubey, in his classic paper "Development of the Hydrosphere and Atmosphere, with Special Reference to Probable Composition of the Early Atmosphere," gives several reasons for his belief about the composition of the early atmosphere. While reading his reasons, notice that they all are based upon some previous assumption concerning either the origin of life or the solar system. He says,

The reasons that have led these writers to consider methane or ammonia, or both, as major constituents of the early atmosphere are probably several, but they may include one or more of the following:

First, we know that hydrogen and helium greatly exceed in abundance all other chemical elements. . . . If hydrogen were at one time very abundant in the atmosphere of the earth, then methane and ammonia, rather than carbon dioxide and nitrogen, should have been the dominant gases.

A second consideration is the fact that methane and ammonia are the most abundant gases in the atmospheres of the major planets. . . .

Third, the hypothesis of Oparin (1938) and Horowitz (1945) is widely attractive to scientists in many fields. This postulates that before ozone became a significant constituent of the earth's atmosphere, complex organic compounds were synthesized by photochemical processes; that the most primitive forms of life originated in this way; and that these first self-duplicating molecules evolved into more specialized organisms. This hypothesis seems to require a reducing atmosphere. . . .

Finally, Miller (1953) has succeeded in synthesizing two amino acids . . . by passing an electric discharge (the effects of which would be comparable to lightning) through a mixture of water vapor, methane, ammonia and hydrogen.[2]

Notice the first two considerations cited by Rubey assume that the earth was formed similarly to the sun and the major planets. If God created the earth, this may be a false assumption and lead to a false conclusion. The second two reasons assume that life evolved out of non-living chemicals and that it did so in a manner similar to Miller's experiment. Once again, if God created life, then Miller's experiment means nothing and the assumption of evolution would be wrong.

Therefore, we can see that the composition of the early atmosphere, which is so critical to the origin of life by evolution, cannot be proven to be as postulated. In fact, in large measure, the supposed composition of the early atmosphere seems to be determined by what it had to have been in order for evolution to occur. No proof is advanced for what it actually was like.

■ NOTES

[1] J. H. Rush, *The Dawn of Life*, Garden City: Hanover House, 1957, p. 79.
[2] William W. Rubey, "Development of the Hydrosphere and Atmosphere, with Special Reference to Probable Composition of the Early Atmosphere," in *The Crust of the Earth*, ed. by Arie Poldervaart, Washington: Geological Society of America, 1955, p. 636.

Does evolution violate the second law of thermodynamics?

There is no need of explaining the origin of life in terms of the miraculous or the supernatural. Life occurs automatically whenever the conditions are right. It will not only emerge but persist and evolve.[1] —Harlow Shapley

In its own way, matter has obeyed from the beginning that great law of biology to which we shall have to refer time and time again, the law of complexification.[2] —Teilhard de Chardin

Such statements are easy to find when one is discussing the origin of life. All one has to do is wait for the right conditions and life will appear. The ease with which these statements are made disguises the difficulties which are encountered when examining the physics of the origin of life. The two writers above, one a respected scientist, the other a famous philosopher, ignore the second law of thermodynamics.

The second law of thermodynamics is a law of

physics. It has governed every chemical, physical or biological interaction ever studied. Basically, the law states that everything tends to run down. Clocks run down; wind-up toys run down; rocks fall down off cliffs but never fall up. In fact, the universe is running down. Physicists tell us that the end of the universe will be cold and black with no light, motion or heat.

The second law of thermodynamics could well be stated as follows:

In any ordered system, open or closed, there exists a *tendency* for that system to decay to a state of disorder, which tendency can only be suspended or reversed by an external source of ordering energy directed by an informational program and transformed through an ingestion-storage-converter mechanism into the specific work required to build up the complex structure of that system.[3]

Another way of explaining this second law is to say that everything tends ultimately to fall apart. Houses deteriorate. Toys break. Certain chemicals spontaneously decompose. Even the diamond in a beautiful ring slowly changes back to black, messy carbon; for a diamond is nothing more than a special form of carbon.

What does all this have to do with the origin of life? Well, if the tendency of all chemicals is to fall apart rather than get more complex, the theory of the chemical evolution of life is in serious trouble and the two statements cited above would be wrong. The second law is a law of simplification, and its work has been observed in every laboratory in the world. It is opposite in effect to de Chardin's "law of complexification."

Scientists constantly talk about how improbable the origin of life is, then state that given eons of time the improbable would become probable and life would arise. However, the second law of thermodynamics indicates that this is not true. Every substance, according to the second law, displays a finite probability of occurrence, but also displays a finite probability of dissolution.[4] Very little is spoken of the probability of break-up of the chemicals being formed by evolution. George Wald writes,

In the vast majority of the processes in which we are interested the point of equilibrium lies far over towards the side of dissolution. That is to say, spontaneous dissolution is much more probable and hence proceeds much more rapidly than spontaneous synthesis.[5]

This means that when the chemicals were "evolving" into life, the long biological chemicals, once synthesized, were far more likely to break up than they were to form. If these chemicals were breaking up faster than they formed, how did enough of them accumulate to form the first cell?

Arthur Eddington notes,

But if your theory is found to be against the second law of thermodynamics I can give you no hope; there is nothing for it but to collapse in deepest humiliation.[6]

The usual approach taken to escape the conclusions of the second law as it applies to the early evolution of life is to claim that the second law is not applicable to the problem since the earth is an "open" system.

Thermodynamics was developed using chemical and mechanical systems which were prevented from either gaining or losing energy or matter with the external world. The earth is receiving energy from the sun all the time and therefore it is claimed that the chemical evolution of life could occur.

Time magazine, criticizing the creationist position on the second law, states,

In 1977 Ilya Prigogine, a Russian-born professor at the Free University of Brussels, won a Nobel Prize in Chemistry for proving that the second law does not apply to "open systems" such as living creatures, because living things can acquire new energy. Plants grow healthy by soaking up sunlight, even though the sun, the source of the solar system's energy, is slowly burning out.[7]

This work of Prigogine's applies only to living systems as they presently are structured.

Photosynthesis is the process by which a plant captures energy from the sun and stores this energy in the form of chemical bonds. When we eat the plant, our bodies utilize the energy to grow bigger and to maintain our present type of body structure. The chloroplast is the motor which captures and directs the sun's energy toward useful work. Burning gasoline does not produce useful work unless there is a mechanism which directs the energy in the proper direction. That function is accomplished by the engine in a car.

When referring to the chemical origin of life, however, we are talking about a time *before* the chloroplast was made; a time before there was a machine which captured, stored and directed the solar energy toward the manufacture of complex compounds. It doesn't matter whether the earth is "open" or "closed" as a system since, without a machine to direct the energy, the chemical evolution of life cannot utilize the solar energy.

Thus as far as the chemicals are concerned, they could just as well be in a closed system, surrounded with solar energy, but with no way to use it. It is much like being on a raft in the ocean with no fresh water. There is water everywhere but not a drop to drink. As George Wald noted,

What we ask here is to synthesize organic molecules without such a machine. I believe this to be the most stubborn problem that confronts us—the weakest link at present in our argument. I do not think it by any means disastrous, but it calls for phenomena and forces, some of which are as yet only partly understood and some probably still to be discovered.[8]

Even in an "open system" Prigogine had reservations about the origin of life. He writes,

The point is that in a non-isolated system there exists a possibility for formation of ordered, low-entropy structures at sufficiently low temperatures. This ordering principle is responsible for the appearance of ordered structures such as crystals as well as for the phenomena of phase transitions.

Unfortunately this principle cannot explain the formation of biological structures. The probability that at ordinary temperatures a macroscopic number of molecules is assembled to give rise to the highly-ordered structures and to the coordinated functions characterizing living organisms is vanishingly small. The idea of spontaneous genesis of life in its present form is therefore highly improbable, even on the scale of the billions of years during which pre-biotic evolution occurred.[9]

The most he said was that he hoped his studies might someday lead to a solution of the problem of the origin of life from non-life. But he acknowledged that we are nowhere near such a solution. He showed that in certain liquid systems, a highly "dissipative" environment might generate some kind of "structure" in one corner of that environment (e.g., vortices in a rapidly heating coffee pot). However, this has been known for a long time, and in no way proves that living systems might emerge from non-living systems simply by placing them in a rapidly dissipating energy milieu.

The very real conflict between evolution and the second law (in open as well as closed systems) is nowhere near to being solved. Even if it were solved in the future, the evolution model still would not be as good as the creation model. That is, at best, the evolution model might possibly someday be able to "explain" the second law in an evolutionary context, but the creation model *predicts* it!

■ NOTES

[1]Harold Shapely, *Science News Letter*, July 3, 1965, p. 10, cited by A. E. Wilder Smith, *Man's Origin, Man's Destiny*, Wheaton: Harold Shaw, 1968, p. 163.

[2]Tielhard de Chardin, *The Phenomenon of Man*, New York: Harper & Row, 1959, p. 48.

[3]Morris, Henry M., *King of Creation*, San Diego: CLP Publishers, 1980, p. 114.

[4]George Wald, "The Origin of Life," *Scientific American*, Vol. 191; 1954, p. 49.

[5]Ibid.

[6]Arthur Eddington, *The Nature of the Physical World*, New York: MacMillan, 1930, p. 74, cited by Bolton Davidheiser, *Evolution and Christian Faith*, Grand Rapids: Baker Bookhouse, 1969, p. 221.

[7]Kenneth M. Pierce, "Putting Darwin Back in the Dock," *Time*, March 16, 1981, p. 81.

[8]George Wald, op. cit. p. 50.

[9]Ilya Prigogine, Gregoire Nicolis & Agnes Babloyants, "Thermodynamics of Evolution," *Physics Today*, Vol. 25, November 1972, p. 23.

Is the DNA stable?

Students constantly are told how small changes in DNA are accumulated in an organism and how these changes gradually alter that organism. This is the raw material of evolution. If one is to believe the radioactive ages, then DNA has been changed at a fast enough rate to change a fish into a man over the past 600 million years. This may sound odd, but if the theory of evolution is true, then our great great great .?.?.?.? grandfather was a fish. Obviously, then, DNA molecules must be changing rapidly. However, some animals have remained the same. This would indicate that the DNA is not prone to changing rapidly—or even at all—over long periods of time.

In looking at these "living fossils" the normally accepted radioactive ages will be cited although the authors do not think they are accurate. They cite them only to illustrate the extreme stability of the DNA molecule.

The nautilus, a deep sea creature, comes to the surface of the ocean only during the night. The nautilus is found in the strata as far back as the Early Cambrian period nearly 600 million years ago. Matthews states,

The nautilus has remained unchanged since the Early Cambrian period.[1]

Thus the DNA of the nautilus has not changed in the last 600 million years.

If the dates are to be believed, the horseshoe crab has remained unchanged for the last 500 million years.[2] The king crab is found, unchanged from today, in strata believed to be over 225 million years old.[3] *Triops cancriformis,* a crustacean, has remained unchanged for over 170 million years[4] while the oppossum has remained unchanged for 75 million years. The Ginkgo tree of Chinese temples has remained unchanged for 200 million years.

Another plant form which has been constant is that of the osmundas. Henry N. Andrews noted,

Among modern plants that deserve the name of "living fossil," the osmundas occupy a place in the foremost ranks. Judging from stem anatomy the extant species and their immediate ancestors have been conspicuous and widespread elements of the earth's vegetation for well over 100 million years.[5]

The coelacanth fish once were thought to have died in the late Cretaceous, yet one was dredged up off of Madagascar in 1938.[6]

Off Central America in the Acapulco trench, a research vessel dredged a living mollusk, once thought to have been extinct over 350 million years ago.[7]

These examples illustrate how stable DNA is if the ages are correct. If DNA is that stable, how can we be sure that evolution has had enough time?

■ NOTES

[1]William H. Matthews, III, *Fossils*, New York: Barnes and Noble, 1962.

[2]E. Peter Volpe, *Understanding Evolution*, Dubuque: W. C. Brown Publishers, 1970, p. 150.

[3]H. G. Wells, Julian Huxley, G. P. Wells, *The Science of Life*, The Literary Guild, 1934, p. 684.

[4]A. H. Sturtevant and G. W. Beadle, *An Introduction to Genetics*, New York: Dover Publications, 1962, p. 263.

[5]Henry N. Andrews, *Studies in Paleobotany*, St. Louis: John Wiley and Sons, 1961, p. 113.

[6]William H. Matthews, III, *Fossils*, p. 256.

[7]H. S. Ladd, "Ecology, Paleontology and Stratigraphy," *Science*, Vol. 129, p. 74.

What are the assumptions of Darwinian evolution?

Frings and Frings[1] list six postulates of the Darwinian view of evolution.

First, Darwin assumed that there was a tendency for animals and plants to reproduce geometrically. By this he meant that a pair of animals had far more offspring than was necessary to replace themselves. A fish may lay millions of eggs in its lifetime. If each egg produced a full-grown adult, the population of that species would swell ominously in a short time.

Darwin's second postulate was that the number of individuals in a species remained relatively constant.

The third postulate was that since large numbers of the offspring failed to reach maturity, there was a struggle or competition for food and reproduction.

Darwin further assumed that there was

variability between individuals and that the variability was unlimited.

The fifth assumption was that natural selection allowed only the "fittest" to survive.

Finally, Darwin assumed that the environment changed continuously so that the definition of what is "fittest" changed with time.

Darwin also believed that the process of change was gradual. He stated:

If it could be demonstrated that any complex organ existed which could not possibly have been formed by numerous successive, slight modifications, my theory would absolutely break down.[2]

Other writers since have departed from the gradual view of evolution and have embraced a more rapid cataclysmic view of how species evolve.

In the next few chapters we will examine these postulates and the speed with which evolution occurs.

■ NOTES

[1] Frings and Frings, *Concepts of Zoology,* New York: Macmillan, 1970, p. 53, 54.
[2] Charles Darwin, *The Origin of Species,* New York: New American Library, 1958, p. 171.

Are mutations advantageous?

The fourth assumption of Darwinian evolution is that the variability in each species is essentially unlimited and that these variations produce beneficial physical traits. If this postulate—or any of Darwin's other postulates—is not true, then evolution could not occur.

A mutation is a change in the structure of the DNA molecule. Since it is a chemical change, it is subject to the laws of physics and chemistry like any other chemical change.

Harold F. Blum observes:

Whatever the nature of mutation, it will have to follow certain lines that are determined by molecular pattern and energetic relationships. Mutation, then, is not random, but may occur only within certain restricting limits and according to certain pathways determined by thermodynamic properties of the system. Thus, to state the case in a somewhat animistic fashion, the organism cannot fit itself to the environment by varying unrestrictedly in any direction.[1]

Thus mutation cannot cause variation in any given direction. This means that if a certain trait is "needed" by an animal for it to survive, the genes might not be able to produce that needed gene because the laws of physics wouldn't allow it. Blum's view of the gene severely restricts the direction in which a creature can evolve.

Even if the laws of chemistry allow the production of a new gene, the odds are that, once produced, the new gene will in reality be detrimental to the organism. A. M. Winchester stated:

Mutation affords virtually unlimited scope for selection. The fact that over 99 percent of the mutations which have been studied in various forms of life are harmful to some degree may seem to rule out the importance of mutation as a factor in adaptive evolution. Yet it is just that fraction of 1 percent which happen to be beneficial that forms the basis for most evolutionary developments. It is because of mutations that life has been able to attain the stupendously complicated organization which many forms now possess. Out of the chaotic mass of random mutations which have occurred through the ages, the phenomena of selection exert their influence and bring order out of chaos.[2]

Even though Winchester wrote fifteen years after Blum's book first appeared, Winchester, ignoring the implications of the laws of physics in limiting variability, still asserts that variability is random. It is not.

Winchester further perpetuates a myth which is passed off as fact by evolutionists: a small percentage of mutations are beneficial to the organism. Dobzhansky says this is not so:

The Classical mutants obtained in Drosophila usually show deterioration, breakdown, or disappearance of some organs. Mutants are known which diminish the quantity or destroy the pigment in the eyes, bristles, legs. Many mutants are, in fact, lethal to their possessors. Mutants which equal the normal fly in vigor are a minority, and mutants that would make a major improvement of the normal organization in the normal environments are unknown.[3]

Not only is mutation and variability limited, no beneficial mutations are known in normal environments. What about the DDT-resistant insects and antibiotic-resistant germs which have been reported in the last few years? Aren't these examples of an improvement in the species?

The answer, unfortunately for evolutionists, is no. Dobzhansky, a committed evolutionist, supplies the answer again. He points out that DDT-resistant flies take longer to develop than normal flies thus reducing the "fitness" of the new strain. He further notes that antibiotic-resistant bacteria also are less fit. He notes:

Why, then, are most colon bacteria found outside of the laboratories still susceptible to bacteriophage attacks and sensitive to streptomycin? Why have the resistant mutants not crowded out the sensitive genotypes? The theory leads us to infer that the resistant mutants must in some respects be at a disadvantage compared to sensitive bacteria in the absence of phages and antibiotics.

This theoretical inference is strikingly verified in some experiments. Close to 60 percent of the streptomycin-resistant mutants in colon bacteria are also streptomycin-dependent; these mutants are unable to grow on a cultural media free of streptomycin. A substance which is poisonous to normal sensitive bacteria is essential for life of the resistant mutants! E. H. Anderson has shown that some bacteriophage-resistant strains of colon bacteria require for growth certain food substances which are not needed for the growth of sensitive bacteria. The resistant mutants will be wiped out in environments in which the required foods are not available.[4]

Thus, even today's examples of "evolution" are, in reality, creatures inferior to the normal variety. This being the case, evolution is really devolution—destruction and breakdown rather than increasing perfection.

The foregoing has shown that Darwin's fourth postulate is invalid. Because of this, evolution itself is invalid.

■ NOTES

[1]Harold F. Blum, *Time's Arrow and Evolution*, Princeton: Princeton University Press, 1968, p. 150.
[2]A. M. Winchester, *Genetics*, Dallas: Houghton Mifflin, 1966, p. 405.

³Theodosius Dobzhansky, *Evolution, Genetics and Man*,
   New York: John Wiley & Sons, 1955, p. 103.
   ⁴Ibid., p. 98.

Is the competition severe within a species?

As shown in a previous chapter, Darwin's
theory pre-supposes that competition for life,
food and mates is most severe between
individuals of the same species. This
competition—believed to be most keen—was
envisioned as the driving force behind
evolution. Only the most fit were theorized to
win the struggle for life. In his section entitled,
"Struggle for Life Most Severe Between
Individuals and Varieties of the Same Species,"
Darwin gives absolutely no examples of this
fierce competition. Subsequent observation has
revealed a phenomenon unknown in Darwin's
time which channels the competitive fighting
into relatively harmless activities.

Territoriality is defined as the tendency of an
animal to hold and defend a territory against all
undesirable intruders of the same species.
Animals which display territoriality include
wolves, dogs, prairie dogs, tigers, fence lizards,
mockingbirds, gibbons, robins, herring gulls,
stickleback fish, the howling monkeys, and
cuckoos, along with many others.

The effects of territoriality in relation to
evolution are two-fold. First, territoriality
spreads the population out so that there is
generally an over-abundance of food in relation

to the population.[1] The second effect of territoriality is that when direct battles between two individuals occur, there are rules.[2] Lethal fighting between two individuals of a territorial species is exceptionally rare. When two enraged animals face each other across their mutual border, they generally will not fight but will engage in displacement activity, an activity totally unrelated to fighting. Two three-spined stickleback fish, when competing over their territory, will chase each other back and forth across the border. Finally, the two enraged fish will come to a halt at their mutual border. Ardrey describes the scene:

And when two male sticklebacks, proprietors of adjoining properties, get into a border uproar and pursue one another back and forth, now on one property, now on the other, to wind up facing each other at the invisible wall bubbling rage and frustrated fury, both will as suddenly as the herring gulls up-end to a vertical position and while goggling at each other, in loathing stand on their heads and dig holes in the sand.[3]

Ardrey points out that this displacement activity is widespread in territorial animals and acts as an outlet for their energy so neither party gets hurt. The roebuck, in a similar border war, will attack and destroy the saplings of the forest. The herring gulls will pull grass; the howling monkey will settle border disputes by, you guessed it, howling.

These activites tend to protect the species from harmful or destructive fighting. Field observations contradict Darwin's assumption of severe competition within a species. J. P. Scott notes:

Animal society in the natural habitat shows very little harmful destructive fighting, even under conditions of great stress, as when . . . subjected to general starvation. On the contrary, such societies exhibit behavior that would in human terms be called co-operative or even altruistic.[4]

If these facts are true, where is the competition which drives evolution? The answer is seen in Darwin's lack of examples of intraspecific competition.

The second implication of territoriality is that the population is spread over an area large enough to support it. A gibbon will control a territory nearly twice as large as is necessary to feed it. The arctic wolf has a territory of about 100 square miles.[5] As we saw earlier, Darwin assumed that the world was over-populated with animals. However, field observation by others since Darwin has shown that the world is not over-populated, at least as far as animals are concerned. Kropotkin observed:

Paucity of life, under-population—not over-population—being the distinctive feature of that immense part of the globe which we name Northern Asia, I conceived since then serious doubts—which subsequent study has only confirmed—as to the reality of that fearful competition for food and life within each species, which was an article of faith with most Darwinists, and consequently, as to the dominant part which this competition was supposed to play in the evolution of new species.[6]

Thus, territoriality reduces the competition which is supposed to drive evolution.

■ NOTES

[1]Robert Ardrey, *The Territorial Imperative*, New York: Dell Publishing Co., 1966, p. 51, 87.
[2]Ibid., p. 81, 82.

[3]Ibid., p. 10.
[4]I. P. Scott reviewing "The Natural History of Aggression"
(a reported symposium, *Science* 148:1965, p. 820, cited by
A. C. Custance, "The Survival of the Unfit," the
Doorway Papers No. 53, Brockville: Privately Published,
1971, p. 18.
[5]Ardrey, op. cit., p. 9.
[6]Petre Kropotkin, *Mutual Aid*, New York: Doubleday, Page
& Co., 1909, p. viii.

Competition or mutual aid?

Competition between individuals of the same
species, as well as between individuals of
different species, is crucial to Darwin's theory
of natural selection. If there is no competition
or struggle for life, there is no reason to
suppose that the fittest survive. Does
observation match the theory?

The idea of competition arose because
Darwin felt that nature was overcrowded, and
that from overcrowding came the competition
for food, nests and mates, and the necessity to
escape from being the prey of another animal.
In this competition, individuals with a slight
advantage over their peers were supposed to
have survived. Two types of competition were
mentioned by Darwin. We will confine ourselves
to discussing the competition between
individuals of the same species, for Darwin
himself felt that here competition would be
more severe. He said:

But the struggle will almost invariably be most severe
between individuals of the same species, for they frequent
the same districts, require the same food, and are exposed
to the same dangers.[1]

In the early 1900s, a Russian prince, Petre Kropotkin, read Darwin's work and investigated for himself, in Siberia and Manchuria, the claim that there was "a terrible competition" between animals of the same species. His book, *Mutual Aid,* reports his findings. He said:

Two aspects of animal life impressed me most during the journeys which I made in my youth in Eastern Siberia and Northern Manchuria. One of them was the extreme severity of the struggle for existence which most species of animals have to carry on against an inclement Nature; the enormous destruction of life which periodically results from natural agencies; and the consequent paucity of life over the vast territory which fell under my observation. And the other was, that even in those few spots where animal life teemed in abundance, I failed to find—although I was eagerly looking for it—that bitter struggle for the means of existence, *among animals belonging to the same species*[2] (his emphasis).

He continued:

Paucity of life, under-population—not over-population— being the distinctive feature of that immense part of the globe which we name Northern Asia, I conceived since then serious doubts—which subsequent study has only confirmed—as to the reality of that fearful competition for food and life within each species, which was an article of faith with most Darwinists, and consequently, as to the dominant part which this competition was supposed to play in the evolution of new species.[3]

He also noted:

. . . that when animals have to struggle against scarcity of food, in consequence of one of the above-mentioned causes, the whole of that portion of the species, which is affected by the calamity, comes out of the ordeal so much impoverished in vigour and health that no progressive evolution of the species can be based upon such periods of keen competition.[4]

Finally, he concluded:

I was persuaded that to admit a pitiless inner war for life within each species, and to see in that war a condition of progress, was to admit something which not only had not yet been proved, but also lacked confirmation from direct observation.[5]

Kropotkin's first chapter contains little else than examples of animals within each species aiding each other. However, instead of citing his examples, we will cite examples of mutual aid between animals of the same species given by Darwin himself.

Darwin cites mutual aid in warning others of danger.[6] Rabbits thump on the ground when danger approaches; horses and cattle warn each other by their stance and attitude; sheep and chamois stomp and whistle. Birds, seals and monkeys post guards. This would not appear to be severe competition.

Darwin further related:

Animals also render more important services to one another: thus wolves and some other beasts of prey hunt in packs and aid one another in attacking their victims. Pelicans fish in concert. The Hamadryas baboons turn over stones to find insects, and when they come to a large one, as many as can stand around, turn it over together and share the booty. Social animals mutually defend each other. Bull bisons in North America, when there is danger, drive the cows and calves into the middle of the herd, whilst they defend the outside. I shall also in a future chapter give an account of two young bulls at Chillingham attacking an old one in concert and of two stallions together trying to drive away a third stallion from a troup of mares. In Abyssinia,

Brehm encountered a great troop of baboons who were
crossing a valley: some had already ascended the opposite
mountain, and some were still in the valley; the latter were
attacked by the dogs, but the old males immediately hurried
down from the rocks, and with mouths widely opened,
roared so fearfully, that the dogs quickly drew back. They
were again encouraged to the attack; but by this time all the
baboons had reascended the heights, excepting a young one
about six months old, who, loudly calling for aid, climbed
on a block of rock and was surrounded. Now one of the
largest males, a true hero, came down again from the
mountain, slowly went to the young one, coaxed him and
triumphantly led him away—the dogs being too much
astonished to make an attack.[7]

Many, many other examples could be cited of
animals of the same species aiding each other.
Even though competition is absolutely critical to
Darwin's theory, Darwin himself knew of many
cases of mutual aid.

■ NOTES

[1]Charles Darwin, *The Origin of Species*, New York: The
   New American Library, 1958, p. 83.
[2]Petre Kropotkin, *Mutual Aid*, New York: Doubleday Page
   and Co., 1909, p. vii.
[3]Ibid., p. viii.
[4]Ibid., p. ix.
[5]Ibid.
[6]Charles Darwin, *The Origin of Species*, and *The Descent of
   Man*, New York: The Modern Library, p. 474-475.
[7]Ibid.

How did these toads evolve?

Darwin's suggestion that evolution came about
through small successive modifications or
changes cannot be applied to every observed
creature. Darwin admitted:

If it could be demonstrated that any complex organ existed which could not possibly have been formed by numerous, successive, slight modifications, my theory would absolutely break down.[1]

We will provide some difficult-to-explain examples. The Surinam toad is mentioned by Wells, Huxley and Wells as an example of how a land-based amphibian solves the problem of no water.[2] The female toad lays her eggs on her back by means of a long oviduct. After the eggs are laid, the skin on her back grows around the eggs and forms a nursery for the young.

One would have great difficulty explaining how such a toad evolved. Perhaps a Darwinian would say that this behavior, and the physiologic structures associated with it, evolved at a time when water was scarce and the need for such behavior was necessary. However, three different phenomena must have evolved or the Surinam toad would have become extinct. First, the long oviduct must have evolved; secondly, the skin of the back must have become capable of surrounding the eggs, or they would have dried out rapidly on the toad's back. Finally, the two physiological structures would have been useless, unless the toad had used them properly.

There is absolutely no reason for either of these structures to have evolved by themselves. A toad with no water to lay its eggs in and possessing only a long oviduct is just as doomed as a toad lacking an oviduct whose back can form a nursery but who is unable to get the eggs onto the back. The offspring of a toad possessing only two of the three needed facilities would die. This is an example of a structure which can't be evolved by small modifications. It all must appear at once or it is useless.

Another toad which also lives in a waterless environment solves the problem differently. The female lays her eggs in the mouth of the male whose vocal sacs become a nursery.[3] Once again, there are several items which must have evolved simultaneously or the whole thing would have been useless. The female must have learned to lay her eggs in the mouth. The male had to evolve behavior which prevented him from eating the eggs, as well as acquiring the ability to change his vocal sacs into a nursery. The lack of any individual item would have doomed the species.

In both of the above cases, the only conceivable impetus to develop these structures would be the drying up of the water in the area in which the toad lived. The toad would not need the structures and behavior millions of years after the water was gone, it would need it *immediately,* before the water was dried up, since the tadpole must develop in a watery environment. The changes must come rapidly or it would be too late.

■ NOTES

[1] Charles Darwin, *The Origin of Species*, New York: New American Library, 1958, p. 171.
[2] H. G. Wells, Julian Huxley, and G. P. Wells, *The Science of Life*, New York: The Literary Guild, 1934, p. 728.
[3] Ibid.

Do embryos show evolutionary development?

One of the most abused pieces of "evidence" for evolution is the idea that an embryo, while it is developing into the adult, reflects the evolutionary heritage of its species. In 1962, William H. Matthews III, professor of geology at Lamar State College, wrote:

A study of the early stages in the development of plants and animals offers additional support of the evolutionary relationship between the simple and the complex forms of life. It is an established fact that animal embryos in their early stages possess structures that resemble structures of the adult forms of less highly developed animals.[1]

Matthews continues by giving the example of "gill slits" in the embryos of amphibians, reptiles, birds and mammals. "Evolutionists," he says, "see these embryonic gill slits as a relic of the past."[2] He further notes:

These and other embryological observations have given rise to the *biogenetic law* or the *law of recapitulation*. This law states that *ontogeny recapitulates phylogeny*—that is, that the development of the individual (ontogeny) recapitulates, or repeats, the development of the race (phylogeny). The biogenetic law appears to agree with studies on the nature of successive growth stages in plants and animals, and it thereby lends support to the theory of organic evolution.[3]

The biogenetic law was first proposed by a German zoologist named Ernst Haeckel in 1869. Haeckel and his followers played an important historical part in the general acceptance of

Darwin's theory of evolution. If it were true that embryos reflected their ancestors, the best explanation for this would be the evolutionary process. However, it has been known since at least 1901 that the biogenetic law has many exceptions and is, in reality, no law at all. In that year, A. P. Pavlov discovered:

The young of certain ammonites possess characters which disappear in the adult stage, while the same characters subsequently reappear in the more highly organized representatives of the same group belonging to species that occur in more recent geological strata.[4]

Leo Berg, in disputing the recapitulation theory, advanced the idea that embryos didn't tell you from where they had evolved but told you only to where they were evolving.[5] He pointed out that in the first stage of development, the embryonic jaws of all mammals are as short as the jaws of man. The brains of embryo birds more closely resemble those of mammalians than of amphibians. This condition persists for a third of the embryo's existence. The chicken embryo's face, he claims, closely resembles that of a human. The amphibian frog tadpole has a beak like that of the bird. These resemblances should not exist if the recapitulation theory is correct.

Most authorities disregard this theory today. Shumway and Adamstone note:

It has been found very difficult, if not impossible, to draw up a geneological tree of the vertebrates based solely on embryological data. Hence, the recapitulation theory is not accepted and applied so unreservedly as formerly.[6]

Dott and Batten admit:

Much research has been done in embryology since Haeckel's day, and we now know that there are all too many exceptions to this simple analogy, and that ontogeny does not reflect accurately the course of evolution. For example we know that teeth developed before the tongue in the vertebrates, yet in the embryo the tongue appears first.[7]

In spite of these facts, almost all paleontologists will speak with authority about the development of the jaw from the gill arches of a fish.[8] A. Lee McAlester, speaking of the origin of the jaw, says:

Comparative studies of fossil agnaths (jawless fish) and placoderm skulls (early fossil jawed fish), combined with observations on the jaw development in the embryos of living vertebrates show that the placoderm jaws probably evolved from the bony supports of the anterior gill of the jawless agnaths.[9]

In light of the above, one must ask whether the use of embryological data on the origin of the jaw is justified.

■ NOTES

[1]William H. Matthews III, *Fossils,* New York: Barnes and Noble, 1962, p. 158.
[2]Ibid.
[3]Ibid.
[4]A. P. Pavlov, "Le Cretace inferieur de la Russe et sa faune," Nouv. Mem. Soc. Nat. Moscov Novv Serie XVI livr. 3 1901, p. 87, cited by Leo Berg, *Nomogenesis,* transl. by J. N. Rostovtsov, Cambridge: MIT Press, 1969, p. 74.
[5]Leo Berg, *Nomogenesis,* p. 108, 109.
[6]Waldo Shumway and F. B. Adamstone, *Introduction to*

Vertebrate Embryology, New York: John Wiley and Sons, 1954, p. 5.

[7]Robert H. Dott and Roger L. Batten, *Evolution of the Earth*, St. Louis: McGraw-Hill Book Co., Inc., 1971, p. 86.

[8]Ibid., p. 263.

[9]A. Lee McAlester, *The History of Life*, Englewood Cliffs: Prentice Hall, Inc., 1968, p. 75.

Are there symbiotic relationships?

Symbiosis—in biology, the living together of two dissimilar organisms in close association or union, especially where this is advantageous to both, as distinguished from parasitism.[1]

Symbiosis is where two animals or plants live in a mutually advantageous relationship. This presents a problem for evolution. Darwin admitted:

If it could be proved that any part of the structure of any one species had been formed for the exclusive good of another species, it would annihilate my theory, for such could not have been produced through natural selection.[2]

Many examples of symbiotic relationships exist. Bolton Davidheiser presents several in his book, *Evolution and Christian Faith*.[3] Douglas Dewar, an anti-evolutionist, relates the case of two wasps, the Sirex and Ibalia. The larva of the Sirex tunnels into the deep interior of a tree. After it changes to the adult form, it tunnels its way to the surface of the tree by means of its powerful jaws. The Ibalia, however, must parasitize the Sirex grub in order to reproduce. The Ibalia will lay its eggs in the hole which the Sirex grub made. The Ibalia larvae then infests the Sirex larva and eats the tissue of the host. Once a Sirex grub is infected with the Ibalia grub, it is doomed. However, the infected Sirex instead of dying in the interior of the tree, where the Ibalia would not be able to escape, bores towards the surface. This instinctive alteration in the Sirex's actions aids the life cycle of the Ibalia, for the Ibalia can escape the tree only if the Sirex dies near the surface of the tree. If the Sirex behaved differently, the Ibalia would be extinct.

A plant and animal in New Zealand also developed a mutually beneficial relationship.[4] The dodo bird ate the leaves of the plant Calvaria Major. The animal got food while the seeds of the plant, passing through the dodo's gizzard, were scratched and became able to germinate. Only the seeds which had been scratched in this manner were able to germinate. When the dodo became extinct, the plant nearly did also. It now can be grown only after the seeds are artificially scratched.

Two examples of the interdependence of forms of life have been presented. Darwin said that proof of interdependence would annihilate his theory. Many others could have been presented, but Darwin (see above) said that only one would be enough to destroy his theory. Why, then is it still accepted? Could it be that people *want* to believe it?

■ NOTES

[1]*Webster's New World Dictionary,* New York: World Publishing Co., 1964, p. 1477.

[2]Charles Darwin, *The Origin of Species,* New York: New American Library, 1958, p. 186-187.

[3]Bolton Davidheiser, *Evolution and Christian Faith,* Grand Rapids: Baker Book House, 1969, p. 200.

[4]Stanley A. Temple, "Plant-Animal Mutualism: Coevolution with Dodo Leads to Near Extinction of Plant," *Science* Aug. 26, 1977, p. 886.

Is the fossil record complete?

Group after group appears in the fossil record without any evidence of evolutionary ancestors. Paleontology attempts to explain this fact by saying that the fossil record is incomplete and that millions of years passed between the deposition of different layers. During these times, new creatures supposedly evolved. This view of an incomplete fossil record is essential if evolution is to be considered a viable theory. Darwin admits:

We have seen in the last chapter that whole groups of species sometimes falsely appear to have abruptly developed; and I have attempted to give an explanation of this fact, which if true would be fatal to my views.[1]

After a century of further searching and examination of the fossil record, many paleontologists are beginning to believe that the fossil record is complete since none of the gaps in the fossil record that existed in Darwin's time has been filled by subsequent study. E. C. Olson observes:

A third fundamental aspect of the record is somewhat different. Many new groups of plants and animals suddenly appear, apparently without any close ancestors. . . . This aspect of the record is real, not merely the result of faulty or biased collecting. A satisfactory theory of evolution must take it into consideration and provide an explanation.[2]

Evolutionists refuse to admit that this lack of transitional forms destroys the theory. Olson wants an explanation of the gaps but I suspect he would not be pleased with the suggestion that the gaps are there because there was no evolution.

There never has been a creature found with half-formed feet or a half-formed wing or feather. If Darwin's idea that all organs and organisms have arisen by slow, small modifications is correct, we should expect fossils like that to appear occasionally. Since the gaps are in the fossil record, these half-evolved monstrosities are postulated to have lived, but not to have been preserved. The gap, it seems, hides their existence.

Is this good—or fair—reasoning? Not really. In truth, it doesn't matter whether the fossil record is complete or not. If it is complete, meaning a large percentage of fossil life has been preserved, then the fossil record does not support evolution. If, however, the fossil record is very incomplete, meaning a small percentage of past life forms have been preserved, what right does science have to fill these gaps with imaginary animals for which there is not the slightest evidence of their existence?

■ NOTES

[1]Charles Darwin, *The Origin of Species,* New York: The New American Library, 1958, p. 316.
[2]E. C. Olson, *The Evolution of Life,* New York: Mentor Books, 1965, p. 94.

Are there transitional forms: creature to creature?

The theory of evolution as originally proposed by Darwin postulated that evolving organisms would gradually change from one type of creature into another over thousands of generations. This implies that there should be gradation in form between a parent and daughter species. A fish would gradually change into a bird. If the species were fossilized and preserved randomly then many transitional forms would be preserved. If this is the case, then the fossil record should reflect this fact.

William H. Matthews III says:

Fossils provide one of the strongest lines of evidence to support the theory of organic evolution. This theory states that the more advanced forms of modern life have evolved from simpler and more primitive ancestral forms in the geologic past. The transformation has been gradual and has been brought about by such factors as heredity, changes in environment, the struggles for existence, and adaptability of the species.[1]

Twenhofel and Shrock state:

No line of evidence more forcefully and clearly supports the fundamental principle of evolution—"descent with accumulative modifications"—than that furnished by fossils.[2]

The important question when studying the fossil record is, does it support the gradual evolution of species? In spite of assurances like those above, the fossil record displays an amazing lack of transitional forms. If these gaps in the record are real, then at least Darwin's

formulation of evolution would be wrong.
Darwin noted:

We have seen in the last chapter that whole groups of
species sometimes falsely appear to have been abruptly
developed; and I have attempted to give an explanation of
this fact, which if true would be fatal to my views. But such
cases are certainly exceptional. . . .[3]

Darwin explained these gaps in the fossil
record by assuming that they represent species
which bridge the gap and yet were not
preserved. Imperfection of the fossil record was
his explanation. However, more than twenty
years of further exploration of the fossil record
has failed to find the needed transitional forms.
E. C. Olson observed:

A third fundamental aspect of the record is sometimes
different. Many new groups of plants and animals suddenly
appear, apparently without any close ancestors. Most major
groups of organisms—phyla, sub-phyla, and even
classes—have appeared in this way. This aspect of the
record is real, not merely the result of faulty or biased
collecting. A satisfactory explanation of evolution must take
it into consideration and provide an explanation.[4]

Thus Darwin's assertion that these cases are
exceptional has not been born out by
subsequent investigations. Many modern
evolutionary theorists have been forced to
propose that evolution does not occur gradually
but occurs suddenly. Thus a species on one side
of the gap is proposed to have given rise
exceptionally rapidly to the species on the other
side. This is of the order of a fish giving birth to
a salamander.

So that you can judge for yourself whether
the fossil record is the best line of evidence for

evolution, statements from paleontologists concerning the shortcomings of the fossil record are listed below.

PLANTS

Supposedly somewhere within the group called algae lay the sources of the higher plants, the vascular groups. Whatever these ancestors may have been, they seem to have been irrevocably lost in the vastness of time.[5]

Land Plants: Since there is considerable question as to just when plants did come from water onto land—estimated dates varying from early Cambrian to Silurian times—it is clear that no one actually knows much about the actual events. There is no tangible evidence whatsoever in the fossil record.[6]

The other three subphyla of seedless plants appear in the fossil record only shortly after the psilopsids, and the very simple structure of the latter suggests that they were ancestral to the others even though no transitional fossils are known.[7]

Both cycads and ginkgoes probably arose from a seed-fern ancestor, but the origin of the remaining gymnosperm group, the familiar conifers with their cones and needle-like leaves, is uncertain.[8]

Somewhere, just a short time before the close of the Age of Reptiles, there occurred a soundless, violent explosion. It lasted millions of years, but it was an explosion nevertheless. It marked the emergence of the angiosperms —the flowering plants. Even the great evolutionist, Charles Darwin, called them "an abominable mystery" because they appeared so suddenly and spread so fast.[9]

ANIMALS

Eight phyla of invertebrate animals have many representatives with mineralized skeletons. . . . Unfortunately, there is no fossil record of the origin of these phyla, for they are already clearly separate and distinct when they first appear as fossils.[10]

Spiders: Much remains to be learned of earlier araneids and of the arachnid group that gave rise to them, since we have no evidence to show that spiders have been derived from any other living or extinct group of arachnids. Nor do we have any conclusive evidence that the arachnids evolved from any arthropod group.[11]

Crinoids: Again, the fossil record is blank at this critical point. The oldest known crinoid, from the very early Ordovician of Europe, has a two-circlet cup, is relatively advanced in many characteristics, and could hardly have been ancestral to many—if any—of the later crinoids.[12]

Coral: The Tetracoralla are considered ancestral to the Hexacoralla, but the exact groups, which were responsible for the ancestry, as well as the time at which the transition from the former to the latter began, is still a speculative matter.[13]

Insects: The Upper Carboniferous period, which witnessed the appearance of reptiles and the decline of the Stegocephalia (amphibians), also gave birth to a considerable population of insects. About a thousand species have been identified, but nothing is known of their past. If they descend from the common stock we have no idea when they branched off to evolve in their own manner.[14]

Speaking of the origin of the vertebrates (animals with back bones), "almost every phylum in the animal kingdom has been suggested including the nemertines."[15]

We have no certain fossil record of lower chordates or chordate ancestors and very possibly never shall have.[16]

Chordates are vertebrates.

Joseph T. Gregory informs us, "One of the best-documented transitions between major classes of animals is the evolution of amphibians from crossopterygian fish.[17] J. Z. Young disagrees saying, "There are such close resemblances between the skulls of the earliest amphibians and those of the devonian crossopterygian fishes that there can be no doubt of the relationship. At present there is, however, no detailed fossil evidence of the stages of transition from the one type to the other."[18]

Salamanders (urodeles): The oldest known salamander is a late Jurassic genus. It is disquieting that even the older fossil salamanders show no primitive characteristics. The modern structural pattern of the urodeles was, it would seem, established by Jurassic time; there has since been little important evolutionary advance.[19]

Frogs: No transitional types, however, are known . . .[20]

Reptiles: An animal known as Seymouria, found in the lower Permian of Texas (perhaps 250 million years old), is of critical importance in our understanding of reptile origins . . . Its characteristics are so exactly intermediate between those of amphibians and reptiles that it is not possible to place it definitely with either group . . .[21]

William Matthes informs us about Seymouria:

It is believed to be a connecting link between these two groups of animals.[22]

However, Seymouria lived in the geologic period after the earliest reptiles, meaning he could not be the ancestor.[23]

Ichthyosaurs (an extinct reptile): The ichthyosaurs appeared suddenly in mid-Triassic time, and no intermediate forms between them and their probable ancestors, the cotylosaurs or stem reptiles, are known.[24]

Lizards: Our knowledge of the early lacertitian radiation is still incomplete, however, and none of the existing lizard families is known before the Cretaceous.[25]

Snakes: The snakes are obviously descended from lizards of some kind, but their precise mode of origin is obscure.[26]

Flying Reptiles: Why, however, the loss of ordinary walking powers should have taken place is not clear. Some light may be shed on this and other problems if ever the missing connecting types, which must have been present in the Triassic, are found as fossils.[27]

Turtles: The exact line of descent of turtles from the step reptiles is not certain.[28]

Marine Reptiles: Most of the later euryapsids, from the mid-Triassic on, are members of well-known, solidly established aquatic groups—nothosaurs, plesiosaurs, placodonts—reasonably considered to be related to one another, but of unknown ancestry.[29]

Dinosaurs: Further, the dinosaurs were not a single group but were already divided at their first appearance into two distinct stocks . . .[30]

Birds and pteradactyls: The Triassic archosaurian reptiles gave rise to two independent stocks that took to the air, the pteradactyls and the birds. Both of these appear first in the Jurassic as animals already well-equipped for flight, although obviously basically of archosauran structure. We, therefore, cannot say anything about the steps by which their flight was evolved and can only speculate about the influences that drove them to take to the air.[31]

Monotremes (egg-laying mammals): The monotremes are mysterious because their ancestry has so far yielded no fossils.[32]

Bats: Except for a few specimens from the Oligocene and Miocene of Europe, we have no record of their history.[33]

Rodents: All attempts to relate the ancestry of the rodents to other groups have been in vain.[34]

Artiodactyls (two-toed grazing animals): Although abundant fossil material is available, the lines of evolution within artiodactyls are not altogether clear and numerous classificatory arrangements have been suggested.[35]

Perissodactyl (one-toed grazers): Right from the very beginning of the known history of mammals, families of the perissodactyls were recognizable. Presumably there had been some differentiation of the different lines before the first known record appeared in the rock.[36]

Marsupials: We know little of the fossil history of these Australian animals . . .[37]

Deer and Cattle: Unfortunately, it is not yet possible to present a connected account of the history of the deer and cattle.[38]

Whales and Porpoises: Like bats, the whales (using this term in a general and inclusive sense) appear suddenly in early Tertiary times, fully adapted . . .[39]

Aardvark: We know little of their fossil history . . .[40]

Prongbuck: There are no apparent ancestors for the prongbucks in the Oligocene or early Miocene of North America.[41]

Seals: As with the two other types, the earless seals may be traced back to the Miocene. Beyond this date, however, our record of pinniped ancestry cannot be traced.[42]

Manatees: Almost nothing is known of the history of the manatees.[43]

Arsinoitherium (a horned fossil mammal from Egypt): This curious creature is quite isolated; we know nothing of its ancestors or of any possible descendants.[44]

Giraffes: The exact origin and affinities of the family remain uncertain.[45]

New World Monkeys: Little is known of the fossil history of these American monkeys.[46]

Old World Monkeys: But they too must go back to unknown Eocene ancestors . . .[47]

Orangutan: Fossil ancestors of the living orangutan of Asia are either unknown or unrecognized.[48]

■ NOTES

[1] William H. Matthews III, *Fossils,* New York: Barnes and Noble, 1962, p. 47.
[2] William H. Twenhofel and Robert R. Shrock, *Invertebrate Paleontology,* New York: McGraw Hill Book Co., 1935, p. 23.
[3] Charles Darwin, *The Origin of Species,* New York: New American Library, 1958, p. 316.
[4] E. C. Olson, *The Evolution of Life,* New York: New American Library, 1965, p. 94.
[5] Ibid., p. 161.

[6]Ibid., p. 160.

[7]A. Lee McAlester, *The History of Life,* Englewood Cliffs: Prentice-Hall, Inc., 1968, p. 89.

[8]Ibid., p. 97.

[9]Loren Eiseley, *The Immense Journey,* New York: Vintage Books, 1957, p. 63.

[10]A. Lee McAlester, *The History of Life,* p. 53.

[11]Willis J. Gertsch, *American Spiders,* Princeton: D. Van Nostrand Co., Inc. 1949, p. 99-100.

[12]James R. Beerbower, *Search for the Past,* Englewood Cliffs: Prentice-Hall, Inc. 1968, p. 401.

[13]Twenhofel and Shrock, *Invertebrate Paleontology,* p. 104, 105.

[14]Lecomte du Nouy, *Human Destiny,* New York: Longmans, Green and Co., 1947, p. 77.

[15]J. Z. Young, The Life of Vertebrates, New York: Oxford University Press, 1962, p. 47.

[16]A. S. Romer, *Man and the Vertebrates,* Baltimore: Penguin Books, 1968, p. 16.

[17]Joseph T. Gregory, "Vertebrates in the Geologic Time Scale", in *The Crust of the Earth,* ed. by Arie Poldervaart, Geological Society of America, Special Paper 62, 1955, p. 602.

[18]J. Z. Young, *The Life of Vertebrates,* p. 356.

[19]Alfred S. Romer, *Vertebrate Paleontology,* Chicago: University of Chicago Press, 1966, p. 101.

[20]Ibid., p. 101.

[21]J. Z. Young, *The Life of Vertebrates,* p. 386.

[22]William Matthews III, *Fossils,* p. 260.

[23]See A. S. Romer, *Vertebrate Paleontology,* p. 95.

[24]Thomas H. Clark and Colin W. Stearn, *The Geological Evolution of North America,* New York: The Ronald Press Co., 1960, p. 346.

[25]J. Z. Young, *The Life of Vertebrates,* p. 404.

[26]Ibid., p. 411.

[27]A. S. Romer, *Vertebrate Paleontology,* p. 147.

[28]A. S. Romer, *Man and the Vertebrates,* p. 116.

[29]A. S. Romer, *Vertebrate Paleontology,* p. 121.

[30]Ibid., p. 148.

[31]J. Z. Young, *The Life of Vertebrates,* p. 426.

[32]William Howells, *Mankind in the Making,* Garden City: Doubleday & Co., 1967, p. 53.

[33]A. S. Romer, *Vertebrate Paleontology,* p. 212.

[34]Edwin H. Colvert, *Evolution of the Vertebrates,* New York: John Wiley & Sons, Inc., 1969, p. 282.

[35]J. Z. Young, *The Life of Vertebrates*, p. 746.

[36]E. C. Olson, *The Evolution of Life*, p. 108.

[37]A. S. Romer, *Man and the Vertebrates*, p. 131.

[38]Charles Schuchert and Carl O. Dunbar, *A Textbook of Geology*, Part II, New York: John Wiley and Sons, 1933, p. 455.

[39]E. H. Colbert, *Evolution of the Vertebrates*, p. 336.

[40]A. S. Romer, *Man and the Vertebrates*, p. 179.

[41]A. S. Romer, *Vertebrate Paleontology*, p. 289.

[42]Ibid., p. 238.

[43]Ibid., p. 254.

[44]Ibid., p. 248.

[45]J. Z. Young, *The Life of Vertebrates*, p. 760.

[46]A. S. Romer, *Man and the Vertebrates*, p. 240.

[47]William Howells, *Mankind in the Making*, p. 100.

[48]D. R. Pilbeam and E.L. Simons, "Some Problems of Hominid Classification," *American Scientist*, Vol. 53, 1965, p. 240.

How are ancestors determined?

Much has been written in paleontological literature concerning various evolutionary lineages. Fish are believed to have evolved into amphibians; amphibians are said to have evolved into reptiles. Reptiles, we are told, evolved into birds and mammals. How is this determined?

When the structure of the various orders of life is surveyed, one fact becomes obvious. Some parts of different animals have a similar function as well as a similar structure. Man has two legs and two arms; so do chimpanzees. Almost every land creature (excluding insect-like animals) has four appendages. Birds have two legs and two wings; dogs have four legs. Almost all animals possess only two eyes.

These are examples of what is called homology.

People long have pondered why these similarities or homologies exist. Theodosius Dobzhansky noted:

The great problem is this: how does homology arise? The solution of this problem was supplied by Darwin: different organisms possess homologous organs because they are descended from a common ancestor. By and large the greater the similarity in the body structure, the closer is the common ancestry; the less the similarity, the more remote is the descent relationship.[1]

Dobzhansky further states:

There is no reason to doubt that similarities between organisms usually indicate common descent, except when the similarities are due to analogy rather than to homology.[2]

Thus what happens in the study of the evolutionary relationships of fossils is the inversion and invalidation of a perfectly logical deduction. If evolution were true, then things which were more closely related would be more similar in structure. This is a logical argument based upon the *assumption* that evolution is true. However, it is not true that when beings are shown to be similar, they are then proven to be close relatives. Similarity means relationship only when it is already assumed that evolution has occurred. Similarity in the structure of various animals cannot be used to prove relationship or evolution.

Similarity in facial structure between two people does not prove that the two individuals are closely related. Hollywood stand-ins usually are similar in appearance to the star, but rarely are related to the star. Other examples like these are easy to find.

The importance of the ability to determine relationship was pointed out by H. H. Newman. He said:

Now a careful survey of the situation reveals the fact that the only postulate the evolutionist needs is no more or less than a logical extension of what the layman considers a truism or self-evident fact, namely that fundamental structural resemblance signifies generic relationship; that, generally speaking, *the degree of structural resemblance runs esentially parallel with closeness of kinship*. Most biologists would say that this is not merely a postulate but one of the best established laws of life . . . If we cannot rely upon this postulate . . . we can make no sure progress in any attempt to establish the validity of the principle of evolution.[3]

Thus we are told that if we can't be sure that resemblance means relationship, neither can we be sure of evolution.

When dealing with fossil material, one must determine relationship solely by the similarities in the two specimens. Unfortunately, similarities don't always mean relationships, even in evolutionary thought. Many similarities are believed to be due to convergence. Convergence is defined as the evolution of similar structures in unrelated or distantly related species. Of course, we are not saying that convergence is an evolutionary phenomenon, but there are cases where similarities exist which aren't due to relationship. David Lack observed:

Australia was colonized by marsupial mammals, which, in the absence of placental forms, evolved into fox-like, wolf-like, mole-like, squirrel-like, rabbit-like, rat-like, anteater-like, and flying squirrel-like forms, which resemble, often closely, their counterparts among the placentals of other continents.[4]

Edwin H. Colbert remarks,

The return of the whales to the sea is a fine example of convergence in evolution. In following this evolutionary trend the whales have shown many adaptions that are remarkably similar to those of the ichthyosaurs, yet the ancestors of these two groups of tetrapods were quite distinct. . . . Convergence such as this illustrates the remarkably similar adaption by dissimilar animals to an environment that imposes stringent limitations upon its inhabitants.[5]

Cases of "convergence" are so easy to find that many have considered it a universal phenomenon. E. C. Olson stated:

In such studies, similar evolution of structures along separate lines, called parallel evolution, is also apparent. This phenomenon, once accorded a rather minor role, has gradually proved to be a pervasive, dominant pattern in many evolutionary transitions between major groups of animals.[6]

Thus, similarity cannot always be considered evidence of relationships and, hence, can't be used to prove evolution. It should also be pointed out that similarities can indicate *common design* rather than common ancestry.

■ NOTES

[1]Theodosius Dobzhansky, *Evolution Genetics and Man,* New York: John Wiley and Son, Inc., 1955, p. 227, 228.
[2]Ibid., p. 234.
[3]H. H. Newman, *Evolution Genetics and Eugenics,* Chicago: University of Chicago Press, 1932, p. 53, cited in Bolton Davidheiser, *Evolution and Christian Faith,* Grand Rapids: Baker Book House, 1969, p. 232.
[4]David Lack, *Evolutionary Theory and Christian Belief,* London: Methuen, 1957, p. 65, cited by Arthur C. Custance, in *Convergence and the Origin of Man,* Brockville: Privately published, 1970, p. 17.

[5]E. H. Colbert, *Evolution of the Vertebrates*, New York: John Wiley and Son, 1969, p. 336, 337.

[6]E. C. Olson, *The Evolution of Life*, New York: The New American Library, 1965, p. 42.

Did the horse evolve?

The alleged evolutionary lineage of the horse is the most famous of all lineages. In any discussion of the evolution of the horse, five neatly schematized states often are presented.

Approximately 50 million years ago, it is believed, a small creature called Eohippus started the horse's evolution. This creature more nearly resembled a hyrax than a horse. The eohippus is believed to have evolved by Oligocene times into a creature called Mesohippus. Mesohippus, in turn, always is shown as evolving into Merychippus who evolves into Pliohippus by the Pliocene epoch, five million years ago. Pliohippus evolved into the modern horse. This, at least, is what we are told.

Several problems attend this tale. First, only five specimens are ever shown. As their size gradually increases, their toes decrease in number until the final horse has only one toe, the hoof. These five specimens are selected from quite a number of possibilities. J. Z. Young says,

The known types of horses are divided into 350 species, but only a small proportion of these can be confidently placed close to the direct line of evolution to Equus (the horse).[1]

In other words, five specimens out of the 350 available have been chosen to be on the direct evolutionary line while the other 345 are never seen.

How did those five specimens come to be chosen? The initial evolutionary lineage of the horse was proposed by V. C. Kowalevsky in 1874.[2] He drew a lineage which included three eastern hemispheric fossil "horses" and the modern horse. This lineage was replaced when H. F. Osborn, former director of the American Museum of Natural History, published his views on the evolutionary lineage of the horse. None of Kowalevsky's specimens is included in Osborn's work, and the four fossil specimens proposed by Osborn are those currently accepted.

One must wonder whether the lineage proposed by Kowalevsky might still be accepted if it weren't for Osborn. It also is probable that entirely different lineages could be constructed out of the available 350 species.

Of Osborn's work, Dott and Batten remark:

Up until recently we were under the illusion that (Osborn's) facts were correct and fully developed. Intensive collecting over the past thirty years has shown that the orthogenetic picture drawn by Osborn is a gross oversimplification. Since our treatment must be brief, we will follow his simple picture, recognizing that the trends are not always consistent within the groups.[3]

Teachers admit that Osborn oversimplifies the picture, yet they present it to their students as fact. The extent of the oversimplification is obvious after reading Young's explanation of how a fossil species is fit into the lineage. He says:

The fossil remains are not usually available in long series of layered beds, such that we can be sure that one population has evolved into the next. However, the dating of fossils can often be done with considerable accuracy by means of the associated animals, and a series can thus be produced such as would be expected in the progress from Hyracotherium to Equus. There are, however, many fossils that show special developments, and cannot be fitted into the direct series. These are presumed to be divergent lines. It must be emphasized that this is an arbitrary, though probably justified, procedure. These "side-lines" are so numerous that they immediately throw doubt on the idea that there has been any single uniform "trend" in horse evolution. At least twelve types sufficiently marked to be classified as genera are known, in addition, to those on the line leading directly to Equus; of course there is a much larger number of shorter independent, evolutionary lines within these genera.[4]

The first problem presented by Young is that these fossils are so scattered around the world no one has any proof that one group could evolve into another. The second problem occurs when one is attempting to fit a specimen into the line. There is no proof that those which don't "fit" are "side-lines" to the main line. Couldn't the five specimens always shown be the "side-lines" and some other set be the main line? Finally, Young admits it is doubtful there has been a uniform "trend" in the horse's evolution. If there isn't this trend, why are we always shown Osborn's uniform oversimplification?

■ NOTES

[1] J. Z. Young, *The Life of Vertebrates*, New York: Oxford University Press, 1962, p. 726.
[2] Bolton Davidheiser, *Evolution and Christian Faith*, Grand Rapids: Baker Book House, 1969, p. 324.
[3] Robert H. Dott, Jr. and Roger L. Batten, *Evolution of the Earth*, St. Louis: McGraw Hill Book Co., 1971, p. 434.
[4] J. Z. Young, *The Life of Vertebrates*, p. 735-736.

Who is man's ancestor?

In 1924, a young anatomist named Raymond Dart discovered the single juvenile skull of what came to be called Australopithecus africanus, which means "southern ape of Africa." Dart projected, from his knowledge of anatomy, that the adult would stand about four feet tall and have the brain-size of a gorilla. When Dart announced his discovery in 1925, the anthropological world rejected his conclusions that his creature was halfway between man and ape. Dart, however, wrote as though everyone believed him.

In 1936, a zoologist turned anthropologist named Robert Broom discovered an adult of Dart's creature and confirmed the previous projections of Dart. From this point, the anthropological world slowly began to accept the idea that Dart's fossil was ancestral to man. By the late 1960s, the view of man's origin was as shown in Figure 1.

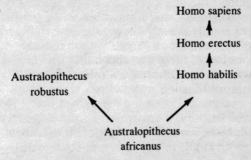

FIGURE 1: THE ACCEPTED VIEW IN THE LATE 1960s AND EARLY 1970s

Australopithecus africanus was believed to have evolved into a creature called Homo habilis and another creature named Australopithecus robustus. Australopithecus robustus was believed to be an evolutionary dead end, but Homo habilis was supposed to have evolved into another creature called Homo erectus who in turn evolved into man.

Speaking of Australopithecus africanus, C. E. Oxnard noted:

For many years now, however, the general concensus has been that these fossils are very close to the human lineage and that particular subgroups . . . are direct human ancestors.[1]

Phillip V. Tobias wrote:

With the wisdom of hindsight, we are today able to recognize in Dart's fossil the first real proof of animal origins of man, the first concrete fossil evidence that Darwin's theory of the origin of species by small modifying steps and gradations from other pre-existing species is applicable to man. For here was an ape-like creature which showed in its anatomical make-up a greater number of resemblances to hominids than are shown by any of the existing man-like apes of Africa or Asia.[2]

Two things strike one about Tobias' statement. First, if Dart's fossil was indeed the first proof of man's evolutionary origin, why were people told that the theory had been proven before the discovery of Australopithecus africanus? Second, Tobias' proof apparently is no proof at all. In physics, or in math, when something is proven, it can't be disproven. In anthropology, things are different. Less than fifteen years after Tobias "proved" that Australopithecus africanus was our ancestor, the bulk of opinion had changed. Today, Australopithecus africanus no longer is considered an ancestor of man.

Three nearly simultaneous occurrences caused the change in opinion. First, C. W. Oxnard published the results of a computer study of the shapes of the bones of Australopithecines, the African apes, and man. For years everyone (as is evidenced by Tobias) exclaimed over how similar man and Australopithecus africanus were. Oxnard proved by mathematical analysis of the bone shapes that Australopithecus resembled apes far more than man. It was claimed that Australopithecus walked upright like man because of certain pelvic features. Oxnard demonstrated that the ankle bones, which are essential for bipedal walking, "differ more from man than the African ape's (ankle bones) do."[3] The African apes cannot walk erect as we do. Apparently neither could the Australopithecines. Australopithecus' foot bones had been reconstructed to show how human-looking its foot was. Oxnard pointed out that a similarly incomplete chimpanzee foot could be reconstructed in the same fashion.[4]

The hand of the Australopithecines resembles the hands of various apes in seven features while resembling the hands of man in only three ways.[5] Oxnard further notes that the shoulder blade fragment, "described many years ago as being rather more like the orangutan than anything else (and this has been confirmed by a recent study) is nevertheless generally treated in discussion as if it were essentially human."[6]

The other two occurrences which overthrew the older view were the discoveries, one by Richard Leakey and the other by Johanson and

White, of more "modern-looking" creatures in supposedly older strata. These two discoveries have led to two competing views of man's origin. Leakey's discovery was interpreted to show that Homo habilis was living at the same time as Australopithecus africanus, Dart's fossil. Thus africanus could not be man's ancestor. This led to the human lineage[7] shown in Figure 2.

Johanson and White's discovery was given a new name, Australopithecus afarensis. This creature is claimed by its discoverers[8] to be the ancestor of Australopithecus and Homo habilis as shown in Figure 3.

Who is correct? No one knows. Further discoveries likely will overturn both of the above viewpoints, and show once again that

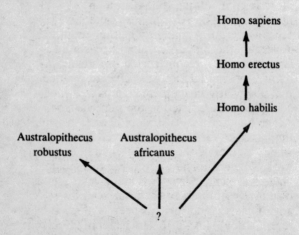

FIGURE 2: RICHARD LEAKEY'S
VIEW OF MAN'S EVOLUTION
A creature called Ramapithecus is believed to have been a distant ancestor which fills the place of the question mark.

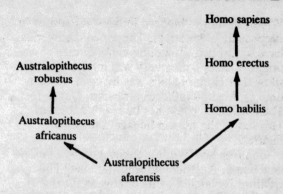

FIGURE 3: JOHANSON AND WHITE'S
VIEW OF MAN'S EVOLUTION It is based upon the
discovery of the fossil named "Lucy."

man's lineage is nothing more than opinion,
which is where it stands today.

There are two different views of man's origin
and no way to tell which is correct—if either is.
Is it really unreasonable to believe that man was
a special creation of God when the science of
anthropology has presented a different
evolutionary lineage for man every ten to
twenty years for the past sixty years?

■ NOTES

[1]C. E. Oxnard, "Human Fossils: The New Revolution," *The
Great Ideas Today, 1977,* Chicago: The Encyclopedia
Brittanica, 1977, p. 142-143.

[2]Philip V. Tobias, "Early Man in East Africa," *Science,* Vol.
149, p. 22.

[3]C. E. Oxnard, "The Place of the Australopithecine in
Human Evolution: Grounds for Doubt?" *Nature,* Vol.
258, p. 389.

[4]Ibid.

[5]Ibid.

[6]Ibid.

[7]Anonymous, "Puzzling Out Man's Ascent," *Time*, Nov. 7, 1977, p. 66, 67.

[8]Donald C. Johanson and Maitland A. Edey, "Lucy" *Science*, March 1981, p. 52.

What is the Hesperopithecus faux pas?

Henry Fairfield Osborn, director of the American Museum of Natural History, opened a package he had received in the mail and found a tooth. But, oh, what a tooth! It had been sent to him by a field geologist named Harold Cook. Cook was inquiring as to what sort of creature the tooth had belonged to.

Osborn took the tooth to his two teeth specialists, Drs. Hellman and Gregory. Both agreed with Osborn's conclusion: Cook had inadvertantly discovered the first evidence of an anthropoid ape in the western hemisphere. In fact, they all three agreed that the tooth more closely resembled the human tooth than does that of any other known ape. They named him Hesperopithecus, ape of the West.

Because of the importance of this discovery, expeditions were organized to find more evidence of this creature. Hellman and Gregory argued over whether the tooth was more ape-like or human. Professor Wilder published a book claiming that Nebraska Man, Hesperopithecus, was halfway between Java Man and Neanderthal Man. Elliott Smith wrote a short article on Mr. and Mrs. Hesperopithecus, including a reconstruction of what they looked like. In all, the discovery created quite a sensation for a period of four-and-one-half years.

The field expedition ran into some difficulty, however. The land-owner upon whose property the tooth had been found refused to allow anyone else on his land. The expedition went to a neighbor's property where they found further evidence of this amazing creature. Hespero-pithecus was a pig. Not in manners, but literally. Hesperopithecus, it turned out, was a peccary—a wild pig!

Is a Piltdown a hoax?

The Piltdown hoax is retold here not to ridicule those involved but to show how the expectation that fossil man should look ape-like can lead to false conclusions. When a person expects a certain event, he can overlook the obvious.

In 1912, William Dawson and A. S. Woodward reported the discovery of an ape-like man in the gravels of the Kent Plateau in England. The fossil skull was broken but was nearly complete and essentially human. The jaw, on the other hand, was very ape-like. Found with the skull were mammal bones, stone tools and an elephant bone ground to a point.

Immediately, some scientists said that the jaw didn't belong to the skull; others asserted equally strongly that it did. As the uproar continued, more excavation was carried out with the result that, at another location, two skull pieces and a single tooth were found.

Since this seemed too much for a coincidence, many who had disputed the original discovery changed their minds and accepted it. This acceptance came in spite of the fact that the tooth in the second find was artificially ground down and that one of the skull fragments appeared to be part of the first skull found. It would be very suspicious indeed for part of the original skull to appear in another find a few miles away. However, these facts were missed.

In 1953, Kenneth Oakley completed some chemical tests on the material. They proved that the skull and jaw did not belong together and that neither belonged with the animal bones. The Piltdown man turned out to be nothing more than a modern human skull with the jawbone of an ape. The material had been chemically treated to make it look old, and the teeth had been filed down to make them look worn. No one knows for sure who the forger was, but he was able to fool modern science for more than forty years. One must wonder why these facts were overlooked for forty years.

Who is Neanderthal Man?

In 1848, at the Forbes quarry at Gibraltar, workmen recovered a fairly complete fossil skull. This skull, as it turned out, was the first Neanderthal skull ever discovered. It also was not recognized as a Neanderthal skull until years after another skull had been discovered and named. In 1856, in a quarry in Germany near the village of Neander, workmen recovered another partial skeleton from the soil in a cave. The skullcap and fifteen skeletal features were given to a Professor

Schlaaffhausen who reported on the find
in early 1857. Since the find had been
made near Neander, the man was called
Neanderthal.

The find immediately became controversial.
Within a few years, the evolutionists would
seize upon Neanderthal as their missing link
between the apes and man. Neanderthal man
was reconstructed to show how he walked with
a stooped gait with his head set far forward.
This appearance gave this man the characteristic
ape-ish look. Since evolution was just then
being proposed, the ape-ish reconstruction lent
support for Darwin's theory.

All was not rosy, however. Several voices
were raised in dissent. Rudolf Virchow, a
pathologist, studied the fossil material and
concluded that the man had had rickets. Francis
Ivanhoe relates:

Nearly a hundred years ago, Virchow diagnosed rickets in
the Neanderthal bones, accounting so for their peculiar
simian cast. Though this was not the first time such an
opinion had been published, it was the first authoritative
statement by one expertly acquainted with the disease who
was also personally familiar with the fossil material. As
other diluvial hominids of the same type turned up in
Belgium and France, the day was carried for Darwinism,
however. Virchow's carefully argued and factual diagnosis
concerning the earlier finds became discredited—by
association, if never objectively. But the growth of
knowledge since, anthropological as well as medical,
suggests that Virchow's views may have been essentially
correct.[1]

Not only did people dissent from the view
that Neanderthal was the intermediate form
between man and ape, fossil finds also disputed
that view. In 1888, the Galley Hill skull, a very

modern-looking skull, was found in strata believed older than Neanderthal. His authenticity was rejected at the time.[2] More modern-appearing discoveries in 1855 at Ipswich, and in 1863 at Abbeville, also were rejected.[3] In 1932 in Kenya, a modern human jaw was discovered in deposits "older" than Neanderthal. Authorities rejected the contemporaneity of the jaw with the deposit.[4] Any time a more modern creature was found, his authenticity was questioned.

In 1939, the first serious attack was made on the view of Neanderthal as an intermediate between ape and man.[5] Professor Sergio Sergi, after studying the skulls of two Neanderthals, proved that they walked erect like we do and not with the ape-like crouch so often depicted. Then in 1947, a Neanderthal was discovered to have lived in a cave after a modern man had inhabited the cave.[6] Thus it was finally proven that Neanderthal was not our ancestor.

Currently, Neanderthal is considered a homo sapiens.[7] His elevation to the status of a man rather than an ape occurred reluctantly in spite of evidence because earlier workers needed Neanderthal as an ancestor.

■ NOTES

[1] Francis Ivanhoe, "Was Virchow Right About Neanderthal?" *Nature*, Vol. 227, p. 577.

[2] J. S. Weiner, "Man's Ancestry," *New Biology* #5, 1948, p. 87, cited in Bolton Davidheiser, *Evolution and Christian Faith*, Grand Rapids: Baker Book House, 1969, p. 162.

[3] Wilhelm Koppers, *Primitive Man and His World Picture*, London: Sheed and Ward, 1952, p. 221, cited in A.C. Custance, *The Influence of Environmental Pressures on the Human Skull*, The Doorway Papers #9, Ottawa: privately published, 1957.

[4] Ashley Montagu, *Man: His First Two Million Years,* New York: Dell Publishing, 1969, p. 79.

[5] A. C. Blanc and Sergio Sergii, "Monte Circeo," *Science,* 90; 1939 supplement, p. 13, cited by A. C. Custance "The Fallacy of Anthropological Reconstructions," the Doorway Papers #33, Brockville: privately published, 1966, p. 7.

[6] A. C. Custance, *The Influence of Environmental Pressures on the Human Skull,* op cit., p. 3.

[7] See J. B. Birdsell, *Human Evolution,* Chicago: Rand McNally & Co., 1972, p. 280.

Is God unscientific?

There are two very basic and opposed philosophical positions concerning the universe: naturalism and supernaturalism. The naturalist assumes that the universe is strictly material, while the supernaturalist says that there are two types of objects in the universe, the natural or material and the supernatural. Both of these viewpoints are accepted as assumptions (and an assumption is accepted or rejected by faith). But once either position is accepted, certain conclusions also must be accepted. For instance, the naturalist assumes that there is no possibility of miracles. Everything in the naturalist's world must be explained on the basis of natural law. This would include the earth, life, and emotions.

The supernaturalist must accept the possibility of miracles since he believes something other than matter exists. And usually he assumes that "other" is a supernatural being. His world can include things that aren't explained on the basis of matter alone. His God, being outside of the material universe, could change the natural law since He authored it.

Science is the study of the material world, and science always is searching for order or laws in the universe. Because of this, it would not do to have God change the natural law every time the scientist entered his laboratory. If God did this, no order ever could be found in the universe. Thus, science must assume God either doesn't exist or He at least does not capriciously change the laws of nature. Experience tells us God does not often interfere with the laws of nature. But can experience prove God *never* interferes in nature, or that He doesn't exist?

As one can see, science must *assume* that God is irrelevant to the operation of the universe on a day-to-day basis before it can insist that any order can be found in the cosmos. Some scientists argue that their natural laws always work; therefore, this consistency proves God has no place in the world. Actually, this line of argument is called a tautology by philosophers. They assume God isn't involved in the universe and then, since their premise is accepted by themselves, they conclude that He really is not involved in it.

Science cannot prove that God is irrelevant to the universe. If God set up the laws of physics, He is hardly irrelevant. If there is no God, then He indeed would be irrelevant. However, each position is accepted by faith. And if each position is accepted by faith, science has no right to throw stones at one who believes in God when the scientist simply chooses to believe differently.

Is fossilization evidence of a catastrophe?

The process of fossilization is itself an evidence of abnormal deposition. Today, when an animal dies, whether on land or sea, the body immediately begins to rot. The scavengers, such as vultures, usually eat the carcass. These two agencies, bacteria and scavengers, are very efficient at recycling the material contained in the body. The bones of the animal will dissolve in the sea or be weathered away on land, so not even the bones are sure to be preserved. Thus, there are two agencies which tend to prevent the fossilization of any animal—biological scavengers and weather.[1]

The only manner in which a carcass can be preserved is to remove it from these two agencies. This means that for an animal to be preserved, it must be buried deep enough so scavengers can't get to it and deep enough so oxygen, which bacteria need, is excluded. This implies, however, that the animal must be buried shortly after its death or there will be nothing left to preserve. As Beerbower states:

In general, the more rapidly an organism is buried and the tighter the seal of its sedimentary tomb, the better the chance of preservation.[2]

Modern sediments do not seem to satisfy the conditions for preservation of fossils. It is very difficult to find creatures currently in the process of being fossilized. Robert J. Cordell notes:

Modern sediments average only about one percent organic matter. . . . [3]

Most of that organic matter is composed of chemicals, not recognizable proto-fossils. Most geologists hold to a view that generally excludes large-scale catastrophes. Their position is that by slow uniform processes, the sedimentary rocks have been deposited and the fossils preserved in them. Their estimates of the rates at which depositional processes occur explain why modern sediments contain such a small percentage of organic material.

J. B. Birdsell estimates that during the last geologic epoch (the Pleistocene), the average rate of deposition was only 0.024 inches per year.[4] If depositional rates like this had prevailed throughout geologic history, and Birdsell contends that they did, then how can there be any fossils at all? As we saw earlier, to preserve an organism, one must bury it deeply—0.024 inch cannot be classified as deep.

Thus it can be seen that the mere presence of a fossil indicates deposition of sediments had to have been thousands of times faster than the normal estimated rates of deposition in order for a fossil to be preserved. If you wished to cover a dead fish with two and one-half inches of sediment, hoping that would be enough to preserve him, you would need a 100-year supply of sediment. And it is uncertain whether two and one-half inches would be deep enough since worms can easily reach that depth and bring the bacteria and oxygen which cause decay. When you look at the major fossil deposits in the world, it becomes obvious that tremendous quantities of sediment were required to preserve them.

Robert Broom, the South African

paleontologist, estimated that there are eight hundred million skeletons of Vertebrate animals in the Karroo formation.[5]

Try to preserve that number of dead animals with only 0.024 inches of sediment and you will utterly fail. Yet that is the average one-year depositional rate.

Other places with fossils—like the Karroo formation—are easily found. The Monterrey shale contains more than a billion fossil fish over four square miles.[6] The Mission Canyon formation of the northwestern states and the Williston Basin are estimated to represent at least 10,000 cubic miles of broken crinoid plates. A crinoid is a deep sea creature. Clark and Stearn conclude:

How many millions, billions, trillions of crinoids would be required to provide such a deposit? The number staggers the imagination.[7]

With these and other examples, is it really reasonable to believe slow deposition preserved these fossils? How much more reasonable to assume they were deposited rapidly in a worldwide flood such as described by the Bible.

■ NOTES

[1]Charles Schuchert and Carl O. Dunbar, *Textbook of Geology*, Pt. 2, New York: John Wiley and Sons, 1933, p. 13.

[2]James R. Beerbower, *Search for the Past*, Englewood Cliffs: Prentice-Hall, Inc., 1968, p. 39.

[3]Robert J. Cordell, "Depths of Oil Origin and Primary Migration: A Critique and Review," *Bulletin of the American Association of Petroleum Geologists*, Vol. 56, p. 2035.

[4]J. B. Birdsell, *Human Evolution*, Chicago: Rand McNally, 1972, p. 141.

[5]N. O. Newell, "Adequacy of the Fossil Record," *Journal of Paleontology*, Vol. 33, May 1959, p. 492, cited by John C. Whitcomb and Henry M. Morris, *The Genesis Flood*, Grand Rapids: Baker Book House, 1961, p. 160.
[6]Ibid., footnote.
[7]Thomas H. Clark and Colin W. Stearn, *The Geological Evolution of North America*, New York: The Ronald Press Co., 1960, p. 88.

Are the fossil deposits environmentally mixed?

If the geologic record is, indeed, the result of slow depositional and erosive forces acting over millions of years, then one should not expect to find animals and plants from widely different environmental zones buried together in one rock stratum. If the fossil record were the result of a world-wide flood, then tropical animals should be expected to be buried with temperate and arctic animals as well as with life from other environments. This would be a good test as to which viewpoint, creation or evolution, was true. By looking in the fossil record, we should be able to tell whether plants are only rarely mixed climatically or if this occurs commonly.

Before examining the evidence, it must be noted that we can say very little about the climate represented by a given animal or plant in fossil strata which contain only extinct forms of life. If none has ever been observed living, we can't tell the habitat.

W. P. Woodring told of a mixed assemblage of mollusks. A mollusk is a class of animals including snails, clams and oysters. Woodring writes,

The Pleistocene marine faunas of California have long attracted attention. Many of them are large: 100 to 350 species of mollusks in one formation. . . . These fauna show different associations. Some associations include cool-water and warm-water species. . . . They evidently do not represent notably different environments . . .[1]

The London Clay flora also show this tendency for plants from diverse environments to be buried together. Andrews reports:

The London Clay flora, of early Eocene age, includes 314 species of seeds and fruits; of this number 234 have been identified whereas the affinities of the remainder are considered doubtful. It is almost exclusively an angiosperm flora, there being but 7 conifers. Of the 100 genera, only 28 are still extant; thus its family relationships will primarily occupy our attention. The present-day distribution of the families which make up the London Clay flora are: 5 are entirely tropical . . . 14 are almost exclusively tropical . . . 21 families are equally tropical and extratropical and five are chiefly temperate.[2]

Wilfred Francis presents many examples of mixed assemblages. He tells of a stratum in England formed mainly from mosses (strictly fresh-water plants), which contains marine animals such as crustacea and fish.[3] Francis remarks:

Such mixed strata are well known features of coal measures of all ages.[4]

The Geiseltal lignites in Germany present a

real problem for the person who doesn't believe in a worldwide flood. Francis wrote:

A similar conclusion is drawn from the evidence of the fossil-bearing layers of the lignites of Geiseltal in Germany. *Here also is a complete mixture of plant, insects and animals from all climate zones of the earth capable of supporting life*[5] (my emphasis).

W.B. Wright, speaking of particular strata, notes:

. . . on top of the arctic freshwater plants and shells is a marine bed. Astarte Borealis and other mollusk shells are found in the position of life, with both valves united. These species are arctic, but the bed seems in other places to contain Ostrea edulis (a mollusk), which requires a temperate sea; the evidence is conflicting as to the climate.[6]

The Chalk Bluffs flora of central California is also mixed environmentally. Andrews observes:

. . . there are some obvious inconsistencies which cannot be overlooked. For example, Artocarpus (breadfruit), Rhamnidium and Tabernae montonae which are tropical genera are associated with temperate climate (hickory, maple, and ash—GRM). This occurrence of climatically divergent elements in a fossil flora is not an uncommon problem . . .[7]

One final example of mixed environmental fossils which frankly amazes this author is found in the Amber beds of East Prussia (Poland). The amber is believed to have been fossilized resin secreted by the ancient trees which lived in the area. Some insects are found encased in the amber, and it is speculated that they got there when the insects, walking on the tree, got stuck and encased in the resin. Later the resin turned to amber. Francis describes what is found in the amber and where it came from. He says:

> Within the lumps of amber are found insects, snails, coral and small portions of plant life. These are of modern type that are now found in both tropical and cold temperature regions. Pine leaves are present, of the types now growing in Japan and North America . . .[8]

Coral? Obviously, the coral was not walking on a tree or in the forest. Coral grows only in the ocean. Therefore, the usual interpretations of how the amber was formed leave much to be desired.

Seven examples of environmentally mixed fossil deposits have been presented. This mixture is what one would expect if the earth had suffered a worldwide flood.

■ NOTES

[1] W. P. Woodring, "Marine Pleistocene of California," Treatise on Marine Ecology and Paleoecology, Vol. 2, *Paleoecology*, H.S. Ladd editor, Washington: The Geological Society of North America, Memoir 67, 1957, p. 594, 595.

[2] Henry N. Andrews, *Studies in Paleobotany*, New York: John Wiley & Sons, 1961, p. 189.

[3] Wilfred Francis, *Coal: Its Formation and Composition*, London: Edward Arnold Ltd., 1961, p. 18, 19.

[4] Ibid.

[5] Ibid., p. 18.

[6] W. B. Wright, *The Quarternary Ice Age*, p. 111, cited by Immanuel Velikovsky, *Earth in Upheaval*, Garden City: Doubleday and Co., Inc., 1955, p. 57, 58.

[7] Andrews, *Studies in Paleobotany*, p. 201, 202.

[8] Wilfred Francis, *Coal: Its Formation and Composition*, p. 17, 18.

Is coal evidence of a flood?

Coal, that black flammable rock, is the result of the compression of large quantities of plant material. It is generally thought that coal formed in huge swamps where plants grew and died, leaving their remains to decay and form a layer of peat on the floor of the swamp. We also are told that as millions of years went by, the layer of peat got thicker and thicker. Finally, the land sank and the swamp was covered by sediment. As more and more sediment was piled on top of the peat, it was further compressed until it became coal.

This view of coal formation, called autochthonous formation (meaning "in the same place"), sees coal as the result of uniform forces acting over millions of years. The plant material would have had to have grown, died and been turned into coal all in the same location.

This view requires several assumptions. First, below the coal would have to be a soil, in which the first plants in the swamp grew. (Sometimes a layer under the coal, called the underclays, is said to be the fossil soil.) Second, all of the plants found in the coal would have to be swamp plants. It would hardly do to have non-swamp plant or animal life found in the swamp. Third, this view would indicate that most of the plant material had decayed fairly effectively, since it was exposed to the elements for a considerable time before being covered by subsequent plant material.

Another view of coal formation, which is not widely accepted today, assumes that the plant material which formed the coal washed in from other localities and then was deposited. This is the allochthonous theory. It states that: (1) there was no soil under the coal, (2) there was non-swamp life in the coal, and (3) there was less decay of the plant material before burial.

These conclusions were arrived at because: (1) if the plants washed into their burial locations, a soil would not have been needed since the plants didn't need it for growth, (2) non-swamp life would be expected to have washed into the burial location along with rocks from other localities, called erratics because they are in an erratic location, and (3) the time between the death of the organism and its subsequent burial was shorter so less decay would be expected.

These are the two main views of how coal was formed. Science now should determine what can be expected from the viewpoints then see which one most nearly fits the facts. Let's examine the facts ourselves and see which viewpoint we feel fits the facts better.

Lenard G. Schultz did an extensive study of the underclays, the supposed soil upon which the pre-coal plants grew. When you dig into the soil today you discover the chemical make-up changing at different depths. This is because the surface soil has been exposed to various chemical processes, known as weathering. The deeper the chemicals, the less they have been affected by weathering. Certain chemicals in the soil are easily destroyed by weathering and thus are a good test of whether an underclay is an old soil. Schultz found that the vertical variations (profile variations) do not coincide

with what would be expected from weathering.
He says:

Chlorite, a mineral easily destroyed by weathering, occurs in
the uppermost parts of underclays. . . . The underclay
profile variations which have been noted do not coincide
with those in modern soils involving a similar mineral
assemblage . . .[1]

Schultz concludes:

Field observations show that underclays were formed before
deposition of coal-forming material began and therefore
cannot be the residual soils on which the coal-forming flora
grew.[2]

The swamp theory of coal formation doesn't
fit the facts in the first test.

The second test of the theories is whether or
not anomalous plants, animals and rocks are
found in coal. Wilfred Francis, in *Coal: Its
Formation and Composition*, tells of many
non-swamp plants found in coal. These include:
pine, sequoia and spruce.[3] Rehwinkle cites
palm, magnolia, poplar, willow, laurel, maple
and birch among other non-swamp plants found
in coal.[4] Thus on the second test the swamp
theory fails.

Clark and Stearn describe what the coal
forests must have been like:

The forest floor must have been a spongy mass of half-
decayed plant matter somewhat like the musket bogs of the
northland today.[5]

This view is not supported by evidence from
the Geiseltal lignites of German. Francis,
speaking of the allochthonous origin (the
washed-from-somewhere-else theory), states:

A similar conclusion is drawn from the evidence of the fossil-bearing layers of the lignites of Geiseltal in Germany. Here also is a complete mixture of plants, insects, and animals from all the climatic zones of the earth that are capable of supporting life. In some cases leaves have been deposited still green, so that the "green layer" is used as a marker during excavations. Among the insects present are beautifully-colored tropical beetles, with soft parts of the body including the contents of the intestines, preserved intact. Normally such materials decay or change color within a few hours of death, so that preservation by inclusion in an aseptic medium must have been sudden and complete.[6]

Thus the uniform view of coal formation fails on all three counts. The description of the Geiseltal lignites by Francis sounds much like what one would expect from a worldwide flood. Is it possible that evidence of a worldwide flood—as spoken of in the Bible—can be obtained from the fact that coals fit the allochthonous (washed in) theory of coal formation?

■ NOTES

[1]L. G. Schultz, "Petrology of Underclays," *Bulletin of the Geological Society of America*, Vol. 69, p. 374.

[2]Ibid., p. 363.

[3]Wilfred Francis, *Coal: Its Formation and Composition*, London: Edward Arnold Ltd., 1961, p. 244.

[4]Alfred Rehwinkle, *The Flood*, St. Louis: Concordia Publishing Co., 1951, p. 197.

[5]Thomas H. Clark and Colin W. Stearn, *The Geological Evolution of North America*, New York: The Ronald Press Co., 1960, p. 123.

[6]Wilfred Francis, *Coal: Its Formation and Composition*, p. 18.

Was the sedimentation rapid?

Is there any evidence in the fossil record to indicate how rapidly the sedimentary rocks were deposited? The importance of this question will be clear once one looks at the estimated rates of deposition. If uniformitarian estimates are anywhere near correct, there never could have been a worldwide flood. One would expect a flood to cause rapid deposition of the sediments, but would expect slow deposition in the absence of a flood.

J. B. Birdsell estimated the depositional rates for three different geologic ages.[1] For one of the more recent ages, the Pleistocene, he says that it took three million years to deposit the 6,000 feet of strata. This works out to approximately 0.024 inch per year. For the Jurassic period, Birdsell's data says the average rate of deposition was around 0.012 inch per year, while for the earliest period, the Cambrian, the average depositional rate was about five thousandths of an inch per year.

One of the first problems with such slow depositional rates is the fact that the process of fossilization would almost never occur. Today, when a creature dies, other animals generally eat the carcass, or else it rots. For an animal to be fossilized, his body must be protected from the scavengers, as well as from the bacteria. This means that the animal must be buried deeply, very quickly after its death, or scavengers or bacteria will attack its body. I would challenge anyone to preserve in an aquarium the body of a dead fish which is covered by only twenty-four thousandths of an inch of mud. The mere fact that fossil fish exist, some exquisitely preserved, testifies that the rates of depostion had to have been faster.

Some fossils irrevocably compel one to the idea that the rates of deposition had to have been faster. Derek Ager, a paleoecologist, said:

In my own collection, I have a lobster from Solenhofen stone of Germany which was apparently fossilized in the act of catching a small fish.[2]

Schuchert and Dunbar report:

A great slab of Hamilton sandstone, found at Mount Marion, New York, and now in the State Museum at Albany, originally preserved the casts of over 400 starfish, some of which died hovering over clams they were in the act of devouring, just as modern starfish eat oysters.[3]

The Eocene Green River formation of Colorado and Wyoming contains a deposit of fine-grained shale with beautifully preserved fossil fish. Matthews says of this:

Probably the best-known fossil-fish fauna is that of the Eocene Green River beds of southern Wyoming and northwestern Colorado. These strata contain large numbers of well-preserved bony fishes.[4]

The Green River formation is a "varved" or banded deposit. Over the 2,600 or so feet of the shale, there are six-and-one-half million bands. Each band is believed to have taken one year to deposit, which if true, would mean it took 6,500,000 years to deposit the entire thickness of the shale. At least this is the usual interpretation of the Green River deposit.

Several features of the Green River tend to contradict the usual interpretation of slow deposition at the rate of one band per year. First, the fossil fish are pressed flat between the bands. Second, one can see the outline of the entire fish, not just the bones. That means the flesh hadn't rotted at the time the fish was buried. Finally, the thickness of each band is such that it would be difficult for a fish to be preserved. The average thickness of a band is about five thousandths of an inch. In the specimen in this author's collection, the bands are approximately one millimeter (one thousandth of a meter or four hundredths of an inch) thick.

What do these facts mean? Well, it is practically impossible for the dead fish to have been preserved if it had been covered by only one millimeter of mud. If one places a dead fish on the bottom of an aquarium and covers him with one millimeter of mud, the fish will rot and float to the surface. Very little decay is seen in the fossil fish of the Green River beds.

Secondly, one millimeter of mud would not provide enough weight to press the fish as flat as they are seen. Thus the only logical explanation for the appearance of the Green River fish is that the entire weight of the formation was laid down rapidly. Only in this fashion could the fish be buried deeply enough to preserve them while also flattening them.

■ NOTES

[1] J. D. Birdsell, *Human Evolution*, Chicago: Rand McNally, 1972, p. 141.
[2] Derek Ager, *Principles of Paleoecology*, San Francisco: McGraw-Hill Book Co., 1963, p. 249.

[3]Charles Schuchert and Carl O. Dunbar, *Textbook of Geology* Pt. 2, New York: John Wiley & Sons, 1933, p. 212.
[4]William H. Matthews III, *Fossils,* New York: Barnes and Noble, 1962, p. 135.

Are footprints evidence of the flood?

All over the world, footprints of various animals are preserved in the fossil record. The usual explanation of how fossil footprints form will not explain all of the facts associated with their existence.

When a person walks across the sand on a beach, or when he walks across a muddy field, he obviously will leave footprints. Immediately following the laying down of the tracks, erosive forces—wind, rain, etc.—begin to destroy the footprints. How long can these tracks remain intact? On a sandy beach or desert sand dune, the wind quickly erases the evidence that anyone had traversed the area. If one walks on a beach in a zone where the waves can cover the tracks, they will be gone after the passage of the first wave. Obviously, tracks are rather ephemeral phenomena.

Because of the fragility of the original tracks, it is obvious that they must be covered quickly or their existence will cease. The only way to keep the tracks long enough for them to be preserved in stone is to cover them with a different kind of material until the sand or mud they are in turns to stone. One does not preserve a footprint in sand by covering the footprint with sand.

Now how does one go about covering a footprint in sand with mud or vice versa? Normal explanations of the fossil record suppose that the whole area sank gradually into the ocean where more sediment was then piled on top of the footprints which turned to stone. However, it is unlikely the footprints could be preserved while sinking because the waves of the ocean would erode them.

Other explanations of preserved footprints suppose that the sand or mud hardened before it sank through the zone of waves. This view ignores the fact that waves easily erode solid rock; how much easier incompletely lithified sand or mud?

As you look at these examples of footprints, ask whether there could be a long period of exposure after the tracks were made before they were either covered or hardened into stone.

Pirrson and Schuchert report:

Of vertebrates higher than fishes, the only evidence rests upon one foot imprint (Thinopus Antiquus) nearly four inches long, which was found near the top of the Upper Devonian of western Pennsylvania. This indicates the presence of a salamander-like animal (stegocephalian) with a probable length of nearly 3 feet. The track is from a marine sandstone of the littoral or beach area over which the animal walked, probably in search of dead marine life. This stratum is associated with others that are ripple-marked and sun-cracked, and bear rain imprints.[1]

Figure 461 in the *Textbook of Geology* by Pirrson and Schuchert shows a preservation in a block of sandstone which would be hard to explain. They say:

Fig. 461—Slab of Trassic sandstone 6 x 3.5 feet, pitted by rain. A large dinosaur (Steropoides diversus) walked over the muddy ground before the storm, and a much smaller one (Argoides minimus) afterwards.[2]

One will notice that raindrops have been mentioned in both of the last examples. The next layer of rock had to be deposited on top of these tracks before the raindrop prints were erased. How long can you see them in the dirt after a rainstorm in your backyard?

The same authors report:

Lea in 1849 collected a most interesting slab, a little over 5 feet long, with six successive series of foot impressions made by an amphibian (Paleosauropus) with a 13 inch stride. This slab is ripple-marked and has rain imprints indicating a mud flat of land origin, over which the animal walked when the deposit was yet soft and wet.[3]

Twenhofel and Shrock report:

Often they record tragedies of the past, such as that found near the German city of Nierstein on the Rhine. Here in the sandstone, which was once a desert sand, are the small tracks of an insect. Death stalks the unwary insect in the form of lizard tracks which converge upon the insect tracks. Soon the two trails come together—and beyond, the lizard walks alone.[4]

Whatever the precise means by which these fossils are preserved, one thing is certain. They must be quickly protected from the erosive forces of the earth or they would not exist. This usually means that the sedimentary layer on top of the tracks had to have been deposited only shortly after the tracks themselves.

One more example will be cited, the Coconino footprints. The Permian Coconino sandstone covers parts of northern Arizona. Certain features in the sandstone indicate it was a dune deposit. Derek Ager reports:

An intriguing feature of the Coconino footprints is that they almost always run uphill on the steeply inclined bedding planes of this dune sandstone.[5]

Why are the animals all running uphill? Why do they not go down? They certainly weren't running from a forest fire in the middle of a desert. Could they have been trying to escape rising flood waters?

■ NOTES

[1] Louis V. Pirrson and Charles Schuchert, *Textbook of Geology*, New York: John Wiley and Sons, 1920, p. 711, 712.

[2] Ibid., p. 826.

[3] Ibid., p. 739.

[4] William H. Twenhofel and Robert R. Shrock, *Invertebrate Paleontology*, New York: McGraw-Hill Book Co., 1935, p. 19.

[5] Derek V. Ager, *Principles of Paleoecology*, San Francisco: McGraw-Hill Book Co., 1963, p. 108.

Where is the clay?

One of the most interesting features of the earth's geologic record is an unconformity, a break in time, between the deposition of two rock strata. During a time of no deposition of sand, clay or limestone, the underlying rocks are eroded, folded, or both (see Figure 1), then more rock is deposited on top of them. An unconformity can be recognized in the field by the angle the lower rocks make with the upper rocks or by the evidence of erosion on the top of a certain stratum.

The generally accepted mechanism for the formation of unconformities requires millions of years. The only way a rock can be laid down is under water and it is initially deposited horizontally. This means that the rocks under the unconformity were laid down under water. Since the only way the rocks can be eroded is above sea level, the rocks laid down under water must be lifted above sea level. After erosion, these rocks must be lowered below sea level again, so a new layer of rocks can be laid down. This entire slow geologic process is said to have taken millions of years.

Many agree that the largest unconformity is a worldwide unconformity which divides the earth's geologic history into two parts. There are practically no fossils below this unconformity, and almost all the fossils of the world are in rocks deposited after this time. Walter S. Olson describes this break in the depositional record:

The phenomena in question are those related to the Cambrian-Precambrian unconformity. This is the most striking and universal break in the succession of rocks covering the earth. The event which they represent has been used to divide the history of our planet into two equal and contrasting parts. The continental nuclei at that time were largely stripped down to the crystalline basement. Ancient mountain systems were worn down to their roots, reducing the continents more nearly to a plain than they have ever been before or since, leaving a clean slate on which the record came to be written which is, usually, called historical geology.[1]

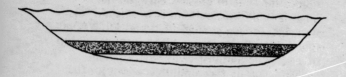

1a. The original sediments are deposited at the bottom of a body of water. They are deposited horizontally.

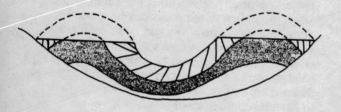

1b. Forces cause the sediments to be folded and eroded.

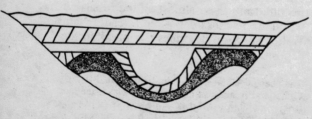

1c. The eroded sediments are once again under water and new sediments are deposited on top of the previously folded sediments.

FIGURE 1: THE DEVELOPMENT
OF AN UNCONFORMITY

Since the time of erosion between the Cambrian and Precambrian is worldwide, the famous American geologist Charles D. Walcott named this time period, which was supposed to have lasted millions of years, the Lipalian Interval.[2] During those millions of years of erosion, no permanent deposition occurred anywhere in the world. That in and of itself appears highly illogical and unlikely. Whenever erosion occurs, the sediment must be deposited somewhere else, or the waters must remain turbulent enough to keep the sediment suspended for millions of years. And yet, if there was sedimentation all over the world, then it is highly unlikely that all areas of sedimentation, worldwide, were re-eroded away.

There is a clue as to what might have occurred if one looks at the rocks deposited immediately after the unconformity. Dott and Batten describe the Cambrian deposits:

Upper Cambrian sandstones, the dominant cratonic sediment, rank among the most mature in the world. They are unrivaled for perfection of rounding and sorting of grains and contain 90 to 99 percent quartz . . .[3]

This high percentage of quartz, a mineral which is the main ingredient of sand, is disturbing to anyone believing that it took millions of years for the deposition of the strata. When the original granite rocks, the source rocks, are weathered, they produce two minerals: clay and quartz. Quartz is the heavier mineral so it *always* is deposited before the clay. Clay particles require very still water for them to be deposited.[4]

However, the rocks observed have almost no clay in them, but the granite source rocks have almost sixty percent clay. Dott and Batten remark:

> Where is all the clay that must have formed by decay of the immense volumes of igneous and metamorphic rocks indicated by the pure quartz sand concentrate? Possible ultimate source rocks contain less than 40 percent quartz, whereas most of the remaining minerals tend to weather to clays.[5]

Remembering that clay requires still waters to be deposited, one can construct a picture of what could have happened geologically from the Cambrian-Precambrian unconformity on. Olson's description of the unconformity sounds much like what one would expect if there had been a worldwide flood such as is described by the Bible. If the erosional period that the unconformity represents lasted only a short catastrophic period, rather than the millions of years currently believed, then the lack of sediments, worldwide, would be reasonable. As the waters calmed, the heavier sand would be deposited, but not the clay since it requires still waters to deposit it. Later, the clay would be deposited.

A flood of worldwide proportions would explain these facts well, since all would have occurred over a very short time span. However, if one desires to believe that the geologic events outlined above took millions of years, then it is up to him to explain why there could be worldwide erosion over millions of years with no deposition. He must also explain how the waters could be kept turbulent enough over millions of years for clay not to be deposited but yet still allow sand to be deposited. In other words, where is all the clay?

NOTES

[1] Walter S. Olson, "Origin of the Cambrian-Pre-Cambrian nonconformity," *American Scientist*, 1966, Vol. 54, No. 4, p. 58.

[2] Thomas H. Clark and Colin W. Stearn, *The Geological Evolution of North America*, New York: The Ronald Press Co., 160, p. 303.

[3] Robert H. Dott, Jr., and Roger L. Batten, *Evolution of the Earth*, St. Louis: McGraw-Hill Book Co., 1971, p. 207.

[4] John Verhoogen et al, *The Earth*, Dallas: Holt Rinehart and Winston Inc., 1970, p. 337 & 405.

[5] Dott and Batten, op. cit., p. 211.

Why don't more scientists accept creationism?

It is fair to ask why more scientists do not accept creationism. Students no longer are taught that there is any evidence which contradicts evolution. Evolution is taught in the universities as though it were a proven fact. Anyone who questions the validity of evolution is automatically suspect in the eyes of the evolutionists. Teilhard de Chardin, an evolutionary philosopher, stated:

Excepting a few ultra-conservative groups it would not occur to any present day thinker or scientist—it would be psychologically inadmissible and impossible—to pursue a line of thought which ignores the concept of a world in evolution.[1]

Teilhard de Chardin has committed the logically fallacious but psychologically effective argument known as the appeal to the people.[2] This fallacious argument tries to win the point by an appeal to emotion. Copi, giving an example of this logical fallacy, says:

Besides the "snob appeal" already referred to, we may include under this heading the familiar "band-wagon argument." The campaign politician "argues" that he should receive our votes because "everybody" is voting that way. We are told that such and such a breakfast food, or cigarette, or motor car is "best" because it is America's largest seller. A certain belief "must" be true because "everyone knows it." But popular acceptance of a policy does not prove it to be wise; widespread use of certain products does not prove them to be satisfactory; general assent to a claim does not prove it to be true. To argue in this way is to commit the ad populum fallacy.[3]

Thus, in looking at what de Chardin said, we find that he called creationists "ultra-conservatives." And obviously no one wants to be that. He also said that you can't be a thinker or a scientist if you don't believe in evolution. These arguments are psychologically powerful and therefore sway a number of people. But they have little to do with whether or not evolution occurred.

D. M. S. Watson, a zoologist, once wrote:

Evolution is a theory universally accepted, not because it can be proved to be true, but because the only alternative, "special creation," is clearly impossible.[4]

Why is special creation impossible? If there is a God and He wanted to create the world, I doubt that Watson's opinion would carry much weight with Him. God could do it regardless of what Watson believes.

E. Peter Volpe wrote:

It scarcely seems necessary to debate the fact that evolution, as an event, has occurred. It is in the *explanation* of evolution that differences of opinion have arisen. One may challenge an interpretation, but to contest the interpretation is not to deny the existence of the event itself. A wide-spread fallacy is to discredit the truth of evolution by seizing upon points of disagreement concerning the mechanism of evolution.[5]

Without presenting any evidence whatsoever that what he says is correct, Volpe has informed his students that: (1) evolution is a fact, and (2) contradictions to evolution can't be used to disprove evolution since these are only disagreements about the mechanism.

Outline a few of evolution's problems to most evolutionists, then watch the reaction. They will probably write you off as a lunatic. Notice the utter disregard for any alternate position as well as the dogmatic affirmation of the evolutionist position in the following statements:

No considerable Christian body, indeed, now insists upon the exact and literal acceptance of the Bible narrative . . .[6] (H.G. Wells, committing the logical fallacy of the band-wagon argument).

The idea of the earth's going round the sun was considered to be just as impious in its time of novelty as was the idea of evolution by the Fundamentalists of the backward States today.[7] (H.G. Wells, Julian Huxley, G.P. Wells, doing some name-calling. Who wants to be backwards?)

Today of course, the belief that living things were especially created for an earth prepared to receive them finds no scientific support.[8]

A student confronted with such opinions is hardpressed to contradict his professor. Since most scientists receive training which ignores any alternatives, is it any wonder that few scientists accept creationism?

■ NOTES

1Teilhard de Chardin, *The Future of Man,* New York: Harper and Row, 1948, p. 85, cited by A.E. Wilder Smith, *Man's Origin, Man's Destiny,* Wheaton: Shaw Publishers, 1968, p. 100.

2Irving M. Copi, *Introduction to Logic,* New York: MacMillan Co., 1972, p. 79, 80.

3Ibid., p. 80.

4D. M. S. Watson, *London Times,* August 3, 1929, cited by Bolton Davidheiser, *Evolution and Christian Faith,* Grand Rapids: Baker Book House, 1969, p. 155.

5E. Peter Volpe, *Understanding Evolution,* 2nd ed., Dubuque: Wm. C. Brown Co. Publishers, 1970, p. xi.

6H. G. Wells, *The Outline of History,* Vol. I, Garden City: Doubleday & Co., 1961, p. 51.

7H. G. Wells, Julian Huxley, G. P. Wells, *The Science of Life,* New York: The Literary Guild, 1934, p. 314.

8J. H. Rush, *The Dawn of Life,* Garden City: Hanover House, 1957, p. 90.

Conclusion

As we travel, we are constantly asked questions about the meaning of life. Who am I? Why am I here? Where am I going? People want to know if there are any answers to life's ultimate questions.

Our response is that there are answers, and these answers are found in the Bible, the inspired Word of God.

This present volume has dealt with reasons we believe skeptics ought to consider Christianity. The book, however, is by no means exhaustive for there are a great many other reasons that could be brought up as to why the Christian faith should be investigated. As it has been in our past works, and as it will be in our future works, we have given some reasons we are firmly convinced the Christian faith is intellectually credible and if a person honestly looks at the evidence Christianity has to offer, he will find a sound basis for placing his faith in Jesus Christ.

Although the evidence is overwhelming as to the validity of the Christian faith, the final proof is left up to the individual who must personally experience it for himself. The Bible says, "Taste and see that the Lord is good" (Psalm 34:8).

As the kings of the earth and the mighty men of the earth are born in exactly the same way physically as the simplest man, so the most intellectual person must become a Christian in exactly the same way as the simplest person.

This is true for all men everywhere, through all space and all time. There are no exceptions. Jesus said in a totally exclusive word: "No man cometh unto the Father, but by me" (John 14:6, KJV) (Francis Schaeffer, *True Spirituality*, p. 1).

Jesus said that to enter the kingdom of heaven a person must be "born again" (John 3:3). This consists of an act of the heart in believing in Jesus Christ as Lord and Savior. When we were born into the world physically, we were born spiritually dead, and therefore we need a spiritual birth. The spiritual birth involves two facets.

The first is to realize that we cannot make it on our own. We are sinners who need help. What is a sinner? A sinner is someone who is separated from God, has chosen to go his own way and cannot get back to God on his own because of his sin.

Sin can be simply characterized as our own self-centered pride and selfishness. More specifically, sin is the violation of a holy God's standard of righteousness.

Thus, we must own up to the fact that we need a Savior, someone who will accomplish all that God requires. The only person ever to do this was Jesus Christ. He lived the only life that was acceptable to God.

He died as a substitute on the cross for our sins, because we have no chance of pleasing God on our own merit. Thus the initial step is to realize that we all have sinned, broken God's law and deserve judgment as a result. The Bible says, "The wages of sin is death" (Romans 6:23, KJV).

Once a person sees his hopeless condition and realizes that Jesus Christ offers an answer, the next step is to receive that offer personally, for "the gift of God is eternal life through Jesus Christ our Lord" (Romans 6:23, KJV). When a person receives Christ as his Savior by accepting God's gift, at that moment he becomes born again.

It is so easy a child can do it, but it is hard because we first have to realize that we cannot do it on our own. Jesus said that to enter the kingdom of heaven a person must be willing to humble himself as a child, and only then will God receive him (Matthew 18:3).

How about you? Have you done this? Have you been born again? If you wish to do it, we offer this prayer that you might pray: "Lord Jesus, I know that I'm a sinner; I realize that I can't make it on my own. Thank You for dying for me. Right at this moment, the best way I know how, I trust You as my Savior and Lord, in Jesus' name. Amen."

If you prayed sincerely to God, then you have become a Christian! One thing which is important to note, though, is that it is not the receiving of the above words which makes the difference. There is nothing magical in them; anyone can repeat a sentence. It is the attitude of your heart and your desire when you pray and trust Christ that makes the difference.

For Further Reading

EVOLUTION

Andrews, E. H., *From Nothing to Nature* (Evangelical Press, 1978). *God, Science and Evolution* (Evangelical Press, 1980). *Christ and the Cosmos* (Evangelical Press, 1986).

Baker, S., *Bone of Contention*. (Evangelical Press, 1986)

Bowden, M., *Ape Men; Fact or Fallacy?* (Sovereign Publications, 1981). *The Rise of the Evolution Fraud?* (Sovereign Publications, 1982).

Cameron, N. M., *Evolution and the Authority of the Bible* (Paternoster, 1983).

Denton, M., *Evolution, a Theory in Crisis* (Burnet Books, 1985).

Morris, H. M., *Science and the Bible* (Scripture Press, 1987).

Whitcomb, J., *The Early Earth* (Baker, 1972).

White, A. J. M., *How Old is the Earth?* (Evangelical Press, 1985).